my **revisi⏻n** notes

Edexcel A2
POLITICAL
IDEOLOGIES

Moyra Grant

Series Editor: Eric Magee

Hodder Education, an Hachette UK company, Carmelite House, 50 Victoria Embankment, London EC4Y 0DZ

Orders
Bookpoint Ltd, 130 Milton Park, Abingdon, Oxfordshire OX14 4SB
tel: 01235 827827
fax: 01235 400401
e-mail: education@bookpoint.co.uk
Lines are open 9.00 a.m.–5.00 p.m., Monday to Saturday, with a 24-hour message answering service. You can also order through the Hodder Education website: www.hoddereducation.co.uk

© Moyra Grant, Eric Magee 2013
ISBN 978-1-4441-8089-3

First printed 2013
Impression number 5 4
Year 2018 2017 2016

Cover photo reproduced by permission of Joef/Fotolia

Typeset by Datapage (India) Pvt. Ltd.
Printed in India

Hachette UK's policy is to use papers that are natural, renewable and recyclable products and made from wood grown in sustainable forests. The logging and manufacturing processes are expected to conform to the environmental regulations of the country of origin.

P2189

Get the most from this book

Everyone has to decide his or her own revision strategy, but it is essential to review your work, learn it and test your understanding. These Revision Notes will help you to do that in a planned way, topic by topic. Use this book as the cornerstone of your revision and don't hesitate to write in it — personalise your notes and check your progress by ticking off each section as you revise.

You can also keep track of your revision by ticking off each topic heading in the book. You may find it helpful to add your own notes as you work through each topic.

☑ **Tick to track your progress**

Use the revision planner on pages 4 and 5 to plan your revision, topic by topic. Tick each box when you have:

- revised and understood a topic
- tested yourself
- practised the exam questions and gone online to check your answers and complete the quick quizzes

Features to help you succeed

Examiner's tips and summaries

Expert tips are given throughout the book to help you polish your exam technique in order to maximise your chances in the exam. The summaries provide a quick-check bullet list for each topic.

Typical mistakes

The author identifies the typical mistakes candidates make and explains how you can avoid them.

Now test yourself

These short, knowledge-based questions provide the first step in testing your learning. Answers are at the back of the book.

Definitions and key words

Clear, concise definitions of essential key terms are provided on the page where they appear.

Key words from the specification are highlighted in bold for you throughout the book.

Revision activities

These activities will help you to understand each topic in an interactive way.

Exam practice

Practice exam questions are provided for each topic. Use them to consolidate your revision and practise your exam skills.

Online

Go online to check your answers to the exam questions and try out the extra quick quizzes at **www.therevisionbutton.co.uk/myrevisionnotes**

My revision planner

Unit 3B Introducing political ideologies

		Revised	Tested	Exam ready
1 Liberalism				
7	Core themes of liberalism	☐	☐	☐
8	The liberal view of government	☐	☐	☐
10	Classical liberalism	☐	☐	☐
11	Modern liberalism	☐	☐	☐
13	Liberal views of equality	☐	☐	☐
14	Liberalism and democracy — how compatible?	☐	☐	☐
15	The influence of liberalism on other major philosophies	☐	☐	☐
2 Conservatism				
17	Traditional conservatism	☐	☐	☐
19	The New Right	☐	☐	☐
23	Comparisons and contrasts within conservatism as a whole	☐	☐	☐
3 Socialism				
25	Core principles of socialism	☐	☐	☐
26	Revolutionary socialism	☐	☐	☐
28	Evolutionary socialism	☐	☐	☐
4 Anarchism				
34	Core principles of anarchism	☐	☐	☐
36	Diverse theories of anarchism	☐	☐	☐
37	Collectivist anarchism	☐	☐	☐
38	Individualist anarchism	☐	☐	☐
38	Other visions of the stateless society	☐	☐	☐
39	Anarchism versus Marxism	☐	☐	☐
40	Anarchism versus liberalism	☐	☐	☐
41	Anarchist strategies and tactics	☐	☐	☐

Exam practice answers and quick quizzes at **www.therevisionbutton.co.uk/myrevisionnotes**

Unit 4B Other ideological traditions

		Revised	Tested	Exam ready
5 Nationalism and racialism				
44	Nationalism	☐	☐	☐
48	Racialism	☐	☐	☐
49	Distinctions and similarities between nationalism and racialism	☐	☐	☐
6 Feminism				
52	'First wave' feminism	☐	☐	☐
53	'Second wave' feminism	☐	☐	☐
56	Contrasts and conflicts within feminist thought	☐	☐	☐
58	Anti-feminism and 'post-feminism'	☐	☐	☐
7 Ecologism				
60	The origins of ecologism	☐	☐	☐
61	Shallow and deep ecology	☐	☐	☐
62	Anti-industrialism	☐	☐	☐
63	Shades of green	☐	☐	☐
64	Ecology and ethics	☐	☐	☐
65	Greens, left and right	☐	☐	☐
8 Multiculturalism				
69	Origins and development of multiculturalism	☐	☐	☐
69	Features of multiculturalism	☐	☐	☐
71	Types of multiculturalism	☐	☐	☐
73	Critical perspectives on multiculturalism	☐	☐	☐

75   Now test yourself answers

Exam practice answers and quick quizzes at **www.therevisionbutton.co.uk/myrevisionnotes**

Countdown to my exams

6–8 weeks to go

- Start by looking at the specification — make sure you know exactly what material you need to revise and the style of the examination. Use the revision planner on pages 4 and 5 to familiarise yourself with the topics.
- Organise your notes, making sure you have covered everything on the specification. The revision planner will help you to group your notes into topics.
- Work out a realistic revision plan that will allow you time for relaxation. Set aside days and times for all the subjects that you need to study, and stick to your timetable.
- Set yourself sensible targets. Break your revision down into focused sessions of around 40 minutes, divided by breaks. These Revision Notes organise the basic facts into short, memorable sections to make revising easier.

Revised ☐

4–6 weeks to go

- Read through the relevant sections of this book and refer to the examiner's tips, examiner's summaries, typical mistakes and key terms. Tick off the topics as you feel confident about them. Highlight those topics you find difficult and look at them again in detail.
- Test your understanding of each topic by working through the 'Now test yourself' questions in the book. Look up the answers at the back of the book.
- Make a note of any problem areas as you revise, and ask your teacher to go over these in class.
- Look at past papers. They are one of the best ways to revise and practise your exam skills. Write or prepare planned answers to the exam practice questions provided in this book. Check your answers online and try out the extra quick quizzes at **www.therevisionbutton.co.uk/ myrevisionnotes**
- Use the revision activities to try out different revision methods. For example, you can make notes using mind maps, spider diagrams or flash cards.
- Track your progress using the revision planner and give yourself a reward when you have achieved your target.

Revised ☐

One week to go

- Try to fit in at least one more timed practice of an entire past paper and seek feedback from your teacher, comparing your work closely with the mark scheme.
- Check the revision planner to make sure you haven't missed out any topics. Brush up on any areas of difficulty by talking them over with a friend or getting help from your teacher.
- Attend any revision classes put on by your teacher. Remember, he or she is an expert at preparing people for examinations.

Revised ☐

The day before the examination

- Flick through these Revision Notes for useful reminders, for example the examiner's tips, examiner's summaries, typical mistakes and key terms.
- Check the time and place of your examination.
- Make sure you have everything you need — extra pens and pencils, tissues, a watch, bottled water, sweets.
- Allow some time to relax and have an early night to ensure you are fresh and alert for the examination.

Revised ☐

My exams

A2 Unit 3B: Introducing political ideologies

Date: . . . .

Time: . . . .

Location:. . . . .

A2 Unit 4B: Other ideological traditions

Date: . . . .

Time: . . . .

Location:. . . . .

1 Liberalism

Liberalism centres on the belief in individual freedom.

There are two broad schools of thought within liberalism:

- Classical liberalism, also known as economic liberalism or neo-liberalism.
- Modern liberalism, also known as social liberalism or welfare liberalism.

Classical liberalism is the older strand, dating from the eighteenth century. Its philosophical priorities are free-market economics and minimal state intervention.

Modern liberalism emerged in the middle of the nineteenth century with philosophers such as John Stuart Mill. It redefined individual freedom to allow for more state intervention and welfare.

Examiner's tip

When questions ask simply about 'liberalism', always address both classical and modern liberalism — usually in that order. However, the balance and emphasis will depend upon the precise theme of the question.

Revision activity

Create two cue cards: one on classical liberalism and one on modern liberalism. These should contain key doctrines, definitions, names and quotes.

Core themes of liberalism

Three key doctrines of liberal philosophy — Revised

- A view of human nature as **rational** but self-interested — an ambivalent view which helps to explain many other liberal doctrines.
- **Individualism:** the rights and interests of every individual are of primary importance.
- **Freedom:** rational individuals are deserving of economic, social and political freedoms.

Typical mistake

Students often describe the liberal view of human nature simply as optimistic, but it is actually quite mixed — liberals believe that humans are rational yet self-serving.

Rationalism — Revised

Liberalism was a product of the Enlightenment — an eighteenth-century 'age of reason'. It rejected earlier beliefs that humans were governed by instinct, emotion and prejudice. Instead, it believes that humans are essentially creatures of reason and logic who base their views and beliefs on evidenced argument rather than on faith and dogma. This gives them the ability and the right to take charge of their own lives and to make their own decisions. **Rational** humans should also be able to resolve disagreements through peaceful discussion and debate without resorting to violence.

Rationalism — the belief that knowledge flows from reason and logic rather than from tradition, custom or faith.

Implications of rationalism:

- individual freedom
- representative democracy
- tolerance
- international peace and harmony

Individualism Revised

Every **individual** is of primary importance, is unique in his or her character and attributes and yet is as important as every other individual. Liberals therefore believe in **foundational equality**: that every individual, despite having different skills and talents, is of equal moral worth and is deserving of the same fundamental human rights. These rival ideas of the uniqueness and equality of every individual have generated tensions within liberal philosophy.

> **Individualism** — a belief in the primacy of the rights and interests of the individual over any group, society or state.

Freedom Revised

A belief in the supreme importance of the rational individual leads logically to an overriding commitment to individual **freedom**. Indeed, for early liberals such as John Locke (1632–1704), it was one of three natural rights — 'Life, liberty and property'. It means that — unlike in feudal times — individuals should make their own decisions about where and how they live, what work they do and what products they buy. 'Over himself, over his own body and mind, the individual is sovereign.' (J.S. Mill) However, this does not mean a licence to harm others.

> **Freedom** — the ability to think or act as one wishes.

Examiner's tip

Point out in essays on liberalism that all liberals believe in the three doctrines described here, but classical and modern liberals interpret them in different ways, as we shall see later.

Now test yourself Tested

1 Explain why the liberal view of human nature is ambivalent.
2 Define 'individualism'.
3 Explain the link between the liberal views on individualism and equality.
4 Why do liberals believe in individual freedom?
5 Give one quotation which expresses the liberal belief in individualism.

Answers on p. 75

The liberal view of government

All liberals subscribe to the **mechanistic model** of state and society. This is the belief that the state is like an artificial machine, created by individuals to serve and protect the freedoms of the individuals within it. These individuals are of equal importance and are effectively interchangeable.

Government is a necessary evil Revised

Liberals believe that government is a necessary evil.

● Government is necessary to protect self-serving individuals from one other.
● Government is evil because it embodies state power, which can be coercive and oppressive.
● 'All power tends to corrupt, and absolute power corrupts absolutely.' (Lord Acton)

- Power corrupts because self-interested individuals will inevitably use it to further their own interests and to oppress and exploit others in the process; and the more power they have, the more they will abuse others.

Limited government

Revised

Liberals therefore believe in limited government. This means that the powers of government should be restricted, legitimate and accountable. All the following doctrines serve to limit the powers of government:

- **Constitutionalism:** there should be a clear and enforceable set of rules which set limits to government power.
- **Rule of law:** every individual should have equal access to the same body of laws and should be equally bound by those laws, which should be fair and impartial.
- **Separation of powers:** the three key functions of the state — legislative, executive and judicial — should be carried out by separate institutions and personnel.
- **Bicameralism:** there should be two houses in the legislature, to check and balance each other.
- **Political and economic pluralism:** there should be diverse and competing power groups in both the economy and the political system — for example, many private enterprises, political parties and pressure groups.
- **Private property:** economic wealth should not be monopolised either by the state or by a few individuals or companies.
- **Consent — representative government:** there should be free, fair and competitive elections to ensure legitimate political authority and accountability.
- **Political equality:** there should be electoral systems based upon one person, one vote, one value.
- **Civil rights and liberties:** there should be legal guarantees of essential rights and freedoms.
- **Decentralisation:** political power should be exercised as close to the individual as possible — preferably by a federal system of government.
- **Equal opportunity:** every individual should have the same access and chance of economic success.
- **Open government and society:** official information should be publicly available, and individuals should have freedom of movement around the country.
- **Negative freedom in the private spheres of home, family and personal morality:** government should not interfere in matters of private moral judgement.
- **Tolerance:** there should be an acceptance, even welcoming, of disagreement, debate and diversity. 'I may not agree with what you say, but I shall defend to the death your right to say it.' (F.M. Voltaire)

Constitutionalism — the belief that government should operate within a constitution — a set of rules which set clear and enforceable limits to its powers.

Consent — the agreement of the people to be governed, granting legitimate authority to the governors.

Tested ☐

6 Define 'constitutionalism' and explain why liberals support it.

7 Define 'pluralism' and explain why liberals support it.

8 In what sphere do modern liberals value negative freedom?

9 Give one quote which illustrates the liberal view of tolerance.

10 Why do liberals experience a conflict of values over attempts to control racism?

11 Which of the checks upon government power listed below are 'external' — i.e. setting limits and boundaries to power; and which are 'internal' — i.e. fragmenting and dispersing power? For each, tick the appropriate column.

Limit to power	External check	Internal check
Constitutionalism		
Bicameralism		
Pluralism		
Rule of law		
Separation of powers		
Federalism		

Answers on p. 75

> **Examiner's tip**
>
> When an essay asks why and how liberals support 'limited government', your answer should focus on the political checks and balances favoured by all liberals, and not on the economic differences within liberalism which are explained below.

Classical liberalism

Classical liberalism is the older strand. Politically, it advocated constitutional government based on consent and the rule of law. Economically, it advocated *laissez-faire*, free-market capitalism. The economic dimension has been abandoned by modern liberals and taken up by neo-liberal conservatives.

The classical liberal view of freedom

Revised ☐

Classical liberals believed in **negative freedom**, i.e. freedom from external interference of any sort, especially by government and state. The state was seen as inherently oppressive and hence as 'a realm of coercion', whereas private or civil society was 'a realm of freedom'. The state was a necessary evil to safeguard law, order and security, but its role should be minimal.

> **Negative freedom** — non-interference; simply being left alone.

John Locke advocated a 'nightwatchman state'; and former US President (1801–9) Thomas Jefferson said, 'That government is best which governs least'. The state should exist only to protect the three natural or inalienable rights of life, liberty and property.

The classical liberal view of the economy

Revised ☐

Above all, classical liberalism believed in *laissez-faire* economics (literally meaning 'leave alone'): free-market, private-enterprise capitalism and the absolute right of the individual to enter and succeed or fail in the market on his own merits, without state help or hindrance. Thus it advocated a free-market economy controlled only by the forces of supply and demand ('the invisible hand' as Adam Smith put it) and not by the 'dead hand' of state regulation or direction. Economic inequality should be an incentive to enterprise. As the American liberal William Sumner put it, 'The drunk in the gutter is just where he ought to be' (1884).

Classical liberals, therefore, believed in 'egoistical individualism' (also sometimes known as 'possessive' or 'atomistic' individualism): a form of individualism which emphasised the self-interested and self-reliant side of human nature.

Revision activity

Devise a table listing at least five contrasts between the doctrines of classical and modern liberalism.

Now test yourself   Tested ☐

12 What is meant by a *laissez-faire* economy?
13 Which philosopher advocated a 'nightwatchman state'?
14 What did Adam Smith mean by 'the invisible hand'?
15 Why do classical liberals favour a substantial degree of economic inequality?
16 Explain what is meant by 'egoistical individualism'.

Answers on p. 75

Modern liberalism

Modern liberalism maintains an emphasis on individual freedom and on constitutional and representative government but now looks favourably upon state economic intervention and welfare.

Revision activity

List ten doctrines of modern liberalism.

The modern liberal view of freedom   Revised ☐

Modern liberalism kept many of the main doctrines of classical liberalism, notably:

● The mechanistic theory of the state.
● A view of human nature as rational and self-interested, therefore corruptible.
● Belief in individual freedom.
● Belief in private property as a natural right.

However, modern liberals came to perceive that negative freedom may penalise individuals who, through no fault of their own, lack the health, education or skills to thrive or even survive unaided. Negative freedom promotes a 'survival of the fittest' system — especially in the free-market economy — and may thus undermine equality of opportunity, social justice, economic efficiency and social harmony.

Examiner's tip

The examiners will be looking for the strongest definitions of 'positive freedom' to refer, primarily, not to the role of the state but to personal flourishing and fulfilment.

The core doctrine of modern liberalism is now positive individual freedom: the actualised freedom to achieve one's own potential and personal development and attain fulfilment, *with* state help and intervention where necessary. The main advocate of this concept was the nineteenth-century liberal T.H. Green (1836–82).

Positive freedom implies, where necessary, a positive and empowering role for state and government, whether in a mixed-market economy

Positive freedom — the actualised freedom to achieve one's own potential and personal development and attain fulfilment, *with* state help and intervention where necessary.

providing health, welfare and education to help individuals to make the most of themselves, or in the state guaranteeing, by law — ideally in a Bill of Rights — freedom from discrimination, freedom of information, freedom of speech and so on.

Typical mistake

Students sometimes define 'negative freedom' and 'positive freedom' as 'freedom from' and 'freedom to', but these definitions are too simplistic and inaccurate.

Revision activity

Suggest three (real or hypothetical) examples of modern liberal policies which would enhance positive freedom.

The modern liberal view of the economy   Revised ☐

Modern liberalism has therefore rejected the free-market economy in favour of a mixed economy with an enabling state providing education, welfare and health services.

This is often described as a Keynesian economy, after the twentieth-century liberal John Maynard Keynes who advocated state intervention and public spending to pull the economy out of depression in the 1930s.

The post-war welfare state in the UK was based on a report by a liberal — the 1942 Beveridge Report — which sought to eradicate the 'five giants':

- want (poverty and hunger)
- disease (sickness)
- ignorance (lack of education)
- squalor (dirt and filth)
- idleness (unemployment)

Modern liberals, therefore, believe in 'developmental individualism': a form of individualism which emphasises humans' capacity and need for personal development and flourishing.

However, modern liberals only advocate welfare as 'a hand up, not a hand out', to enable individuals to become self-reliant. They stop well short of the extensive 'cradle-to-grave' welfare state supported by many socialists.

Revision activity

Imagine that you are writing two election leaflets. Write a paragraph for each: (a) as a classical liberal, explaining why you are strongly against state welfare, and (b) as a modern liberal, explaining why you support state welfare.

Examiner's tip

When exam questions ask, 'to what extent' do classical and modern liberals disagree about freedom, remember to mention that they all agree on non-intervention in the private moral sphere of home and family.

Now test yourself   Tested ☐

17 List four doctrines which modern liberalism inherited from classical liberalism.
18 What is the main difference between classical liberalism and modern liberalism?
19 What do modern liberals see as the proper role for the state?
20 Give three examples of how the liberal state may promote positive freedom.

Answers on p. 75

Examiner's tip

When an essay asks why and to what extent liberals favour 'state intervention', your answer should focus upon the economic role of the state and the limits to that intervention advocated by classical and modern liberals respectively.

Liberal views of equality

Three forms of equality

Revised

All liberals believe in three forms of **equality**, but classical and modern liberals interpret the last one differently:

- **Foundational equality**: all individuals, simply by virtue of being human, are of equal moral worth and are equally deserving of fundamental human rights.
- **Formal equality**: (i) legal equality — the rule of law; (ii) political equality — one person, one vote, one value.
- **Equality of opportunity**: equal access and chance for economic success. Classical or economic liberals interpret this in terms of negative freedom: individuals should be equally left alone to succeed or fail on their own merits. Modern or social liberals interpret it in terms of positive freedom: disadvantaged and deprived individuals should be given help by the state in the form of education, welfare or health services to provide a 'level playing field'.

All liberals reject the socialist doctrine of equality of outcome, because it treats unalike individuals alike and is therefore unjust.

> **Equality** — humans are of equal worth, should be treated the same way and should receive fair and equitable rewards.

> **Typical mistake**
>
> It is a mistake to over-emphasise liberalism's advocacy of equality. All liberals believe that economic inequality is an incentive to effort and a reward for merit, and all liberals prioritise freedom.

Now test yourself

Tested

21 List three forms of equality advocated by liberal thought.

22 Why do liberals reject the socialist idea of equality of outcome?

23 Look at the liberal doctrines below. In each case, tick the appropriate column to indicate whether they are features of classical liberalism or modern liberalism.

Liberal doctrine	Classical liberalism	Modern liberalism
Free-market economy		
Egoistical individualism		
Developmental individualism		
Welfare		
Positive freedom		
Negative freedom		

Answers on p. 75

> **Examiner's tip**
>
> To help you with essays which ask you about liberal views for and against equality, construct a two-column table putting arguments for on one side, and arguments against on the other.

Liberalism and democracy — how compatible?

How compatible?

Although the political socialisation of most Western students leads them to assume that '**liberal democracy**' is the only valid form of democracy, many forms of democracy are not, in fact, liberal (e.g. direct democracy, and the various one-party systems such as communist democracy, third-world democracy and fascist-totalitarian democracy). Moreover, early liberals were downright hostile to the idea of democracy even in its fairly limited form of 'one person, one vote'.

> **Liberal democracy** — a form of representative government based on free, fair and competitive elections, pluralism, constitutionalism, the rule of law, civil liberties and a (free- or mixed-) market economy.

> **Typical mistake**
>
> Some students make the mistake of asserting that liberalism is unequivocally in favour of democracy. This takes too narrow a view of both liberalism and democracy.

Liberals' wariness of democracy

All liberals are wary of democracy because:

- Democracy is collectivist.
- Democracy implies majoritarianism — 'tyranny of the majority'.
- Democracy may therefore undermine individual sovereignty and minority rights.
- Democracy may give a voice to the uneducated, the ignorant and the propertyless.
- Democracy may threaten property rights.
- Democracy implies equality over freedom.
- Democracy may generate growing state intervention and control.
- Democracy may limit economic freedom and growth.
- Democracy may produce dangerously powerful demagogues (e.g. Hitler).
- All power, even 'people power', tends to corrupt innately self-seeking humans.

Liberals' support for democracy

However, modern liberals favour democracy because:

- Power should be based upon legitimate authority.
- Consent is necessary for such legitimacy.
- The people can be a constraining influence upon the power of government and state.
- Democracy may help to ensure political representation.
- Democracy may enhance pluralism — diffusion of power between competing groups.

- Democracy may be used to enhance civil liberties.
- Democracy may be educative.
- Democracy may promote individual self-development.
- Democracy may allow conflicting interests in society to be mediated and reconciled.
- Democracy may promote social harmony and stability.

Modern liberals have, therefore, come to embrace democracy, but only in its specifically liberal form. They reject other forms of democracy — which may be less pluralist or more participatory — as downright dangerous.

Examiner's tip

When essays ask about the extent of liberalism's compatibility with democracy, it is best to explain their wariness of democracy first and then to explain why they favour democracy; because on balance liberals are now staunch advocates of democracy, in its liberal form.

Now test yourself

Tested ☐

24 Define 'liberal democracy'.
25 Why might the concept of 'liberal democracy' be a contradiction in terms?
26 Give two reasons why liberals are wary of democracy.
27 Give two reasons why liberals favour democracy.

Answers on p. 75

Typical mistake

When asked why liberals favour liberal democracy, students often answer simply in terms of the liberal belief in freedom, but stronger answers refer firstly to the liberal belief in human rationality.

The influence of liberalism on other major philosophies

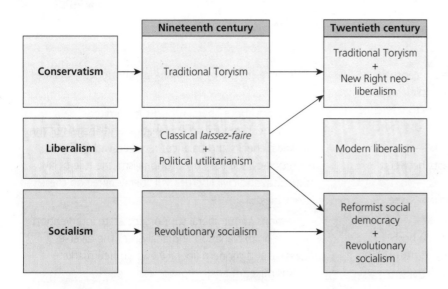

Figure 1.1 Influence of liberalism on conservatism and socialism in the nineteenth and twentieth centuries

Liberalism's influence on conservatism

Revised ☐

The Conservative Party, through the rise of Thatcherism, has adopted the free-market economics and atomistic individualism of classical liberalism — i.e. New Right neo-liberalism.

Liberalism's influence on socialism

Post-war, reformist social democracy was influenced more by liberalism than by socialism, and advocated a mixed, Keynesian economy — much like modern liberalism, but not individualist.

'New' Labour adopted a liberal form of communitarianism, in that its emphasis on widening individual rights and entitlements was balanced against a stress on social duty and moral responsibility. Its welfare reform policies were influenced by this rights-and-responsibilities agenda. 'New' Labour's constitutional reforms were — in diluted form — largely derived from constitutional liberalism with its belief in decentralising and fragmenting power.

Now test yourself

28 Which sub-strand of conservative thought has been most influenced by liberal ideas?

29 Which sub-strand of Labour Party thought has been most influenced by liberal ideas?

Answers on p. 76

Exam practice

A Short-answer questions

1 Distinguish between economic liberalism and social liberalism.

2 Why and how have liberals supported the fragmentation of political power?

3 Why have some liberals warned against the dangers of democracy?

B Essay questions

4 'Power tends to corrupt and absolute power corrupts absolutely.' Explain, and discuss the implications of this view for liberalism.

5 'Liberal democracy is a contradiction in terms.' Discuss.

6 'The similarities between classical liberalism and modern liberalism are greater than the differences.' Discuss.

Answers and quick quiz 1 online

Examiner's summary

✔ Short questions often focus upon one conceptual strand within liberal thought — for example, freedom, equality or rationalism — but it may be with reference only to modern liberalism or it may be across liberal theory as a whole.

✔ Short questions may ask about contrasts between liberal and conservative or socialist views — for example, about human nature or equality — see Chapters 2 and 3.

✔ References to 'economic liberalism' include both nineteenth-century classical liberalism and twentieth-century (New Right conservative) neo-liberalism.

References to 'social liberalism' mean modern, welfare liberalism.

✔ Questions about liberal support for 'limited government' require an explanation and analysis of the political checks and balances required within liberal democracy, such as constitutionalism, the rule of law, pluralism and civil liberties. All liberals agree on these doctrines.

✔ Questions about liberal support for 'state intervention' require an explanation and analysis of the diverse classical and modern liberal views on free-market versus mixed-market economies.

2 Conservatism

There are two broad schools of thought within modern conservatism:

1 Traditional political conservatism, or Toryism.
2 New Right or 'Thatcherite' conservatism. This, in turn, has two sub-strands within it:

   (a) neo-liberal economics
   (b) neo-conservative social authoritarianism

Traditional Toryism is the older strand, dating from Edmund Burke (1729–97). Its philosophical priorities are social stability, order and harmony through a resistance to change.

The New Right came to the fore in the 1970s. Their philosophy is rooted in classical liberal free-market economics, combined with social authoritarianism in all other spheres.

> **Examiner's tip**
> When questions ask simply about 'conservatism', always address both Toryism and the New Right — usually in that order.

Traditional conservatism

Two key doctrines   Revised ☐

There are two key doctrines of traditional conservative philosophy:

1 the organic theory of society and the state
2 a mistrust of human nature: it is morally, psychologically and intellectually imperfect

The organic theory of society and the state

The **organic theory** likens the state to a living organism — like a tree or a human body — with its parts unequal and interdependent (leaf versus roots or hand versus brain). The whole is greater than the sum of its parts, and the state is more important than the individual within it (just as the leaf needs the tree for its survival, but not vice versa). Thus the individual owes a duty of loyalty and obedience to the state, upon which he depends for his survival. There is a natural, harmonious hierarchy within society, i.e. the organic theory believes that inequality is inevitable and desirable.

> **Examiner's tip**
> When exam questions ask why conservatives object to social equality, your answer should focus upon the organic model of society.

Mistrust of human nature

Traditional conservatism is 'a philosophy of human imperfection' (Noel O'Sullivan) in three distinct senses.

1 **Conservatives have traditionally viewed human beings as psychologically imperfect** — as limited, dependent and security-seeking creatures who seek identity and rootedness. This implies a resistance to change and helps to explain why conservatives value tradition and cultural homogeneity.

2 **Human beings are morally imperfect** — in accordance with the doctrine of original sin, they are greedy and selfish creatures, motivated by base impulses and desires. This implies the need for a strong state, firm law and order and the moral guidance of the church.

3 **Human beings are intellectually imperfect** — the world is too complex for them to explain and understand rationally or logically. This implies that abstract theories and principles are not to be trusted and helps to explain why history, tradition, experience and pragmatism are the surest guides to human action. However, the New Right neo-liberals reject this view: they endorse human rationalism and therefore have faith in abstract theory and believe in negative economic freedom and individual self-reliance.

> **Typical mistake**
>
> It is too strong to say that traditional conservatives think humans are 'irrational'. Rather, they think that there are limits to human reason.

> **Now test yourself**   Tested ☐
>
> 1   For each of the three imperfections of human nature below, suggest three conservative doctrines or principles that follow.
>   ● intellectual imperfection
>   ● moral imperfection
>   ● psychological imperfection
>
> Answers on p. 76

> **Examiner's tip**
>
> When exam questions ask how traditional conservatives and the New Right disagree in their view of the individual, your answer should focus upon the contrasting views of human nature, and should not digress onto their contrasting views of society.

Other central themes   Revised ☐

The two key doctrines above, in turn, explain the other central themes of traditional conservatism:

● private property
● tradition
● natural hierarchy and authority
● a static, harmonious class structure
● pragmatism
● paternalism

Tradition

Conservatives value **tradition** for the following reasons:

● The organic society reaches out into both past and future and cannot be severed from its roots if it is to survive.
● Intellectually imperfect humans should look to tradition and history as guides to action, rather than to human reason and abstract theories.
● Tradition — including cultural history — can provide a sense of identity, security and stability for psychologically imperfect humans.
● From a pragmatic perspective, if something has survived for a long time, it clearly works. 'What has stood the test of time is good and must not be lightly cast aside.' (Edmund Burke)

> **Tradition** — an institution or practice which has existed for a long period of time and therefore embodies stability and continuity.

> **Typical mistake**
>
> Some students make the mistake of explaining the conservative reverence for tradition purely in terms of Toryism's resistance to change. Stronger answers link Tory support for tradition to the organic model of society and to humans' intellectual and psychological imperfection.

Authority

Conservatives value **authority** for the following reasons:

● Authority is an essential feature of the organic and hierarchical structure of society, where the 'natural governors' make the key decisions in the common interests of the whole society.
● Authority is a form of social glue which binds psychologically insecure people together and gives them a sense of rootedness, identity and stability.

> **Authority** — rightful, legitimate power.

- Since human nature is morally flawed, only the exercise of authority from above can prevent a descent into chaos and disorder.
- Conservatives have tended to link authority to wisdom, in that, by training and accumulated experience, those in authority come to know 'what is best' for everyone — implying paternalism.

Traditional conservative 'one nationism'

The traditional conservative desire for 'one nationism' arose from nineteenth-century Conservative PM Benjamin Disraeli's fear of a growing economic divide between rich and poor — 'two nations' — and of consequent social unrest and disorder. His solution was (limited) welfarism to help the poorest in society.

This Tory **paternalism** is not premised upon the pursuit of either equality or freedom, but upon a pragmatic desire to prevent social rebellion and hence to preserve the power and privileges of the 'natural governors'. As Disraeli said, 'If the cottages are happy, the castle is safe': that is, some degree of caring for the poor will prevent social unrest or even revolution, and will ensure that the social stability of the natural **hierarchy** — and the dominant position of the ruling class — is maintained.

Tory paternalism is also premised upon a concept of *noblesse oblige* — a duty of social compassion towards those who are at the bottom of the natural, God-given, organic hierarchy through fate and not through any fault of their own.

Conservatives have thus supported 'one-nation' principles for both **pragmatic** and moral reasons. The pragmatic basis for one nationism is the fear that widening social inequality — the 'two nations' of rich and poor which Disraeli feared — will threaten the established order by fuelling pressure for social revolution. The moral case for one nationism rests in paternalism, a belief in guidance and support being exercised for the benefit of those who cannot act in their own best interests.

Because of its pragmatism, Toryism does not perceive itself as a doctrinaire ideology — but it does, nevertheless, have clearly identifiable theoretical principles, such as the organic theory and mistrust of human nature.

The New Right

Also commonly known in the UK as 'Thatcherism', this has two different, and potentially conflicting, sub-strands within it: New Right **neo-liberalism** and New Right neo-conservatism.

New Right neo-liberalism ————————————————— Revised

The roots of **neo-liberalism** lie in nineteenth-century classical liberalism. Therefore it involves:

- **mechanistic**/individualist **theory**
- a view of human nature as rational and self-seeking
- radical and reactionary thinking
- free-market economics (negative economic freedom)

Paternalism — benign authority exercised by the natural governors to guide and support those below — implying a form of anti-egalitarian welfarism, also known as 'one nationism'.

Hierarchy — static, structured inequality where an individual's position is not determined by ability or effort.

Pragmatism — a practical and flexible response to changing circumstances rather than an adherence to abstract, rigid theory and principles.

Typical mistake

It is a mistake to describe 'one nationism' as traditional conservative support for nationalism and/or patriotism (although they do support these sentiments as well). 'One nationism' means traditional conservative support for paternalist, organic welfarism.

Now test yourself

2 Why is Toryism anti-egalitarian?
3 Why do conservatives value the nation?
4 Why do Tories value tradition?

Answers on p. 76

Tested

Neo-liberalism — a contemporary version of classical liberal theory which favours a free-market capitalist economy and minimal state intervention.

Mechanistic theory holds that the state is like an artificial machine, created by man to serve man, with its parts interchangeable, and therefore the individual is the unit of primary importance — more important than any group or the state itself.

- **libertarianism**
- principled and doctrinaire thinking

The neo-liberal view of society is of atomistic individualism, meaning that that individuals are more important than society; that individual rights and freedoms should take priority over duties and social obligations; and that the economy should allow equality of opportunity, allowing individuals to rise and fall on the basis of merit with no help or hindrance from the state. As Margaret Thatcher famously said, 'There is no such thing as society — only individuals and families'.

> **Libertarianism** — advocacy of negative freedom and minimal state intervention.

Revision activity

Draw two model diagrams to illustrate your understanding of the organic and the mechanistic views of society (for example, a pyramid and a ladder).

Why has the New Right advocated rolling back the state?

It is the neo-liberal strand of the New Right which advocates rolling back the state. By this they mean, seeking to minimise the state's intervention in the economy.

Reasons:

- They believe that the free market is self-regulating and will establish its own equilibrium, which state interference would disrupt.
- High taxation violates property rights, undermines individual incentive and enterprise and amounts to legalised theft.
- High public spending fuels inflation.
- Nationalised industries amount to state monopolies and are inefficient and uncompetitive.
- State welfare is both inefficient and immoral because it undermines self-reliance and individual responsibility, and promotes a 'dependency culture' and a 'nanny state'.

Neo-liberalism is principled rather than pragmatic because it has faith in human reason and hence in theory. As Thatcher said, 'No U-turns — the lady's not for turning'.

Neo-liberalism is, above all, rooted in the belief that free-market capitalism promotes economic well-being in that it is self-regulating, and it serves as a form of social discipline, imposing economic constraints upon the working class. This *laissez-faire* or libertarian position also reflects a deep fear of the state based on the perceived threat it poses to individual rights, particularly property rights, and its tendency towards growth and excessive power.

What is new about New Right conservatism is that, to its neo-liberal, *laissez-faire* economic dimension, it has added a political, social and moral authoritarian dimension in all non-economic spheres. This does not derive from the paternalism of Disraeli but from an earlier, reactionary and highly disciplinarian school of organic conservatism espoused by, for example, nineteenth-century French writer Joseph de Maistre. This has been labelled 'neo-conservatism'.

> **Examiner's tip**
>
> When exam questions ask why the New Right advocates 'rolling back the state', they mean, why does neo-liberalism want to push state intervention out of the economy.

> **Examiner's tip**
>
> Exam questions often ask how and why conservatives value tradition, but remember that not all schools of conservatism are traditionalist; neo-liberalism is anti-traditional because it draws on rationalist theories and assumptions.

> **Now test yourself**
>
> 5   Describe the traditional conservative view of human nature.
> 6   Describe the New Right neo-liberal view of human nature.
> 7   Give one quote from Thatcher to illustrate neo-liberal individualism.
> 8   Define 'pragmatism' and explain why Tories value it.
> 9   Why do New Right neo-liberals reject pragmatism?
> 10 Give one quote from Thatcher to illustrate this point.
>
> Answers on p. 76
>
> Tested

> **Examiner's tip**
>
> When exam questions ask you to distinguish between the traditional conservative and the New Right views of society, focus upon organicism versus atomistic individualism; do not digress onto their diverse views of human nature.

Exam practice answers and quick quizzes at **www.therevisionbutton.co.uk/myrevisionnotes**

New Right neo-conservatism

Revised

Neo-conservatism involves:

- organic/collectivist theory
- natural hierarchy and authority
- mistrust of human reason
- reactionary thinking
- illiberal and **authoritarian** thinking
- principled and doctrinaire attitudes

Whereas traditional conservatives are organic paternalists, neo-conservatives are organic authoritarians, whose solution to social instability and disorder is punitive discipline — e.g. strict law and order — rather than benevolent welfarism.

> **Neo-conservatism** — a contemporary version of authoritarian social conservatism which advocates strict law and order, exclusive nationalism and traditional family values.
>
> **Authoritarianism** — advocacy of strong, centralised control from above, coercive if necessary.

Typical mistake

Students often wrongly define 'reactionary' as 'reacting to circumstances'. It means 'seeking to turn back the clock and return to an earlier situation which is perceived as better than now'.

Conservative views

Revised

Conservative views on social change

- **Traditional conservatives:** favour tradition, continuity and limited change to conserve.
- **Neo-conservatives:** favour substantial reactionary social change.
- **Neo-liberals:** favour radical and reactionary economic change.

Conservative views on human nature

- **Organic conservatives:** intellectually imperfect, psychologically imperfect, morally imperfect.
- **Neo-liberals:** rational, independent and self-reliant, self-interested and egoistic.

Conservative views on society

- **Traditional conservatives:** paternalist organicism.
- **Neo-conservatism:** authoritarian organicism.
- **Neo-liberalism:** atomistic individualism.

Conservative views on moral and cultural diversity

Organic conservatives — both traditionalists and neo-conservatives — fear moral and cultural diversity because of their assumptions about society and human nature.

- For conservatives, society has an organic character in that the whole is more than the collection of its individual parts. Society is thus bound together by a fragile network of relationships and institutions. Order and stability within such societies is promoted by shared values and a common culture; moral and cultural diversity therefore threaten conflict and even social breakdown.
- Moreover, as human beings are morally limited and psychologically dependent creatures, shared values and a common culture are vital

Examiner's tip

When explaining conservative views of human nature, point out that there is some overlap of views on human self-interest and egoism; otherwise they starkly contrast.

Revision activities

- Imagine that you are writing two election leaflets. Write a paragraph for each: (a) as a traditional conservative, explaining why you support state welfare, up to a point; (b) as a neo-liberal, explaining why you are strongly against state welfare.
- Suggest three (real or hypothetical) examples of neo-conservative policies on law and order.

sources of rootedness and belonging, helping to engender a stable and secure sense of identity. Cultural and moral diversity are thus also associated with rootlessness and personal insecurity.

- However, this perspective is not shared by neo-liberals, who value moral diversity and multiculturalism.

Examiner's tip

Almost all essay answers on conservatism will need three sections: one on traditional conservatism, one on neo-liberalism and one on neo-conservatism.

The New Right 'paradox' — Revised

A primary goal of the neo-liberal New Right is a return to the free-market economy which dominated the classical liberal, Victorian era of the nineteenth century. Thus, unlike traditional conservatism, it is both radical and reactionary: it seeks a lot of change, backwards. However, it has allied this *laissez-faire* economic doctrine to an equally reactionary authoritarianism in all other (non-economic) spheres of life, which makes it internally contradictory:

Table 2.1 The New Right 'paradox'

Neo-liberalism	Neo-conservatism
Mechanistic theory	Organic theory
Rationalist	Mistrust of human nature
Negative economic freedom	Illiberal
Equality of opportunity	Anti-egalitarian
Limited state	Strong state

'Limited but strong' government

Quotations summarising the New Right paradox of 'limited but strong' government include:

- 'Limitation of government doesn't make for a weak government. If you've got the role of government clearly set out, then it means very strong government in that role. Very strong indeed.' (Margaret Thatcher)
- 'What this country wants is less tax and more law and order.' (Margaret Thatcher)
- 'The trouble with a free-market economy is that it takes so many police to make it work.' (Neal Ascherson)

These quotes, in their different ways, all imply that the economic libertarian and political/social authoritarian dimensions of New Right thinking are not so much paradoxical as complementary — two sides of the same coin. The free market of the 1980s and 1990s resulted in growing economic inequalities and social disorder, which required stronger policing and political controls to keep the lid on potential social unrest.

Revision activity

Create three cue cards: one on traditional conservatism, one on neo-liberalism and one on neo-conservatism. These should contain key doctrines, definitions, names and quotes.

Typical mistake

When essay questions ask about the internal coherence of the New Right, it is a mistake to write more than a brief introductory mention of traditional conservatism.

Now test yourself — Tested

11 Give one key difference between traditional conservatism and neo-conservatism.

12 Summarise the New Right 'paradox'.

13 Why might these New Right views actually be perceived as complementary?

14 Give one quote which illustrates this view.

Answers on p. 76

Comparisons and contrasts within conservatism as a whole

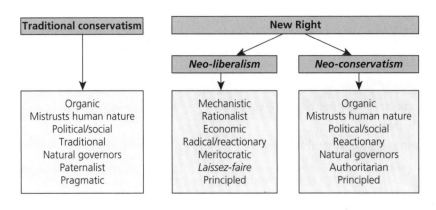

Figure 2.1 Comparisons between traditional conservatism and the New Right's neo-liberalism and neo-conservatism

There seems to be more in common between traditional conservatism and neo-conservatism, than between neo-liberalism and neo-conservatism (i.e. within the New Right). However, all conservatives share a few common beliefs.

Examiner's tip

Essay questions often ask whether there are more similarities or differences across conservatism as a whole. The neo-liberal school is the most distinctive of the three schools of thought within conservatism.

Shared conservative beliefs — Revised

Tories and the New Right share a common belief in four main things:

1 Private **property** — although the neo-liberal emphasis on the free market and on unconstrained property rights is much stronger than the Tories'.

2 Hierarchy — although there is a clear difference between the Tory perception of an organic, static, class hierarchy and the neo-liberal mechanistic, individualist ladder of meritocracy.

3 Law and order — although the paternalist, Tory 'Dixon of Dock Green' image of the bobby on the beat contrasts sharply with the militaristic, neo-conservative 'Robocop' version of policing.

4 Christian family values — again, paternalist compassion versus authoritarian discipline.

Property — the ownership of wealth or material goods, whether by individuals, groups or the state.

Typical mistake

It is a mistake to say that traditional conservatives regard private property as a right, in the way that neo-liberals do. For traditional conservatives, private property is about duties and responsibilities.

How do conservatives justify private property?

For traditional and neo-conservatives:

● Property provides psychologically insecure humans with a sense of security and safety.

● Property ownership encourages morally imperfect humans to respect other people's property and to be law-abiding.

● Property can reflect its owner's personality.

For neo-liberal conservatives:

● Property is a natural right (said John Locke).

● Property is an incentive to individual effort.

● Property is a reward for individual merit.

Revision activity

Devise a plan — either a written bullet-point summary or a mind map — for the following 45-minute essay title: 'To what extent have conservatives preferred pragmatism to principle?'

15 Give two similarities between traditional conservatism and neo-conservatism.

16 How does the traditional conservative view on private property differ from the neo-liberal view?

17 How does the traditional conservative view on inequality differ from the neo-liberal view?

18 Why do organic conservatives value law and order?

19 Which philosopher asserted private property as a natural right?

20 For each of the following quotations, give the name of the person who said it and suggest what aspect of conservative philosophy it illustrates.

(a) 'Traditional conservatism is a philosophy of human imperfection.'

(b) 'What has stood the test of time is good and must not be lightly cast aside.'

(c) 'If the cottages are happy, the castle is safe.'

(d) 'There is no such thing as society — only individuals and families.'

Answers on p. 76

Exam practice

A Short-answer questions

1 Why does traditional conservatism claim that it is not an ideology?

2 Why has the New Right advocated rolling back the state?

3 How do traditional conservatives and the New Right differ in their views of society?

B Essay questions

4 'Conservatism is a philosophy of human imperfection.' Discuss.

5 Has conservatism been more concerned with social stability than with economic freedom?

6 To what extent is the New Right internally coherent?

Answers and quick quiz 2 online

Online

Examiner's summary

✔ Short questions often focus on one school of conservative thought; essay questions usually require comparisons and contrasts across the three schools of conservatism — Toryism, neo-liberalism and neo-conservatism.

✔ When questions ask about the conservative view of human nature, answers should explain the three 'imperfections' and the implications of each of them — for example, tradition, private property, law and order. Short questions about, for example, the conservative view on human nature or society, will only require a couple of lines about the different neo-liberal view; essays will require a much more balanced contrast.

✔ Essays on the diverse schools of conservative thought should not merely describe the differences, but should explain why they often strongly oppose each other, by reference to their core doctrines on human nature and society.

✔ Some questions — even short answers — may include different exam topics, for example 'Distinguish between a conservative and a socialist view of human nature' (see next chapter).

3 Socialism

Socialism is probably the most wide-ranging of all the political philosophies. Very broadly, it can be sub-divided in two alternative ways:

1 The end goals of socialism:

   (a) 'Fundamentalist socialism' seeks to abolish capitalism entirely.

   (b) 'Revisionist socialism' merely seeks to reform and tame capitalism.

2 The means of achieving socialism:

   (a) 'Revolutionary socialism' seeks mass working-class uprising.

   (b) 'Evolutionary socialism' seeks to pursue the parliamentary, ballot-box road.

Each of these broad categories has, in turn, many sub-strands.

> **Socialism** — a philosophy which believes in human altruism and seeks varying degrees of equality, common ownership and collectivism; whether by revolution or by the parliamentary route.

> **Examiner's tip**
>
> When exam questions ask simply about 'socialism', always address both revolutionary and evolutionary socialism — usually in that order.

Core principles of socialism

Core principles
`Revised`

- A view of human nature as **rational and altruistic** — that is, as having concern for the welfare of others. (This contrasts with the liberal view of human nature as rational but self-interested.)

- **Egalitarianism:** a belief in far-reaching equality of outcome — probably the defining doctrine of socialism.

- **Collectivism:** a belief that humans work best — that is, most ethically and efficiently — in cooperative social groups rather than as self-striving individuals.

- **Social justice:** a fair distribution of wealth, income and social status, which for socialists means greater equality, pursued collectively. (This contrasts with the liberal view of social justice which is based on individualism and meritocracy.)

- **Social harmony:** a society based on collectivism and equality would be a recipe for social cohesion and community.

- **Democracy:** the belief that rational and altruistic humans are deserving of 'people power', whether in direct or indirect/representative form.

> **Typical mistake**
>
> The socialist belief in equality does not mean that they think all humans are identical in abilities or needs; rather that material inequalities in capitalism are not fair or just.

> **Typical mistake**
>
> 'Collectivism' is not just the opposite of 'individualism'; nor does it only mean common economic ownership, which is more precisely called 'collectivisation'.

> **Examiner's tip**
>
> When answering questions about why socialists favour equality, it is important to address human altruism, collectivism and the socialist belief that inequalities in capitalism are the fault of the economic system and not of the poor and deprived themselves.

Why do socialists believe in social equality?

- Socialists believe that economic inequalities in capitalism are the result of systemic injustices.
- Equality would enhance positive freedom by safeguarding people from poverty and allowing them to flourish and fulfil their potential.
- Without social equality, other forms of equality — e.g. foundational and formal equality — are not possible. Socialists argue that liberals are deluding themselves on this point.
- Social equality would enhance social harmony and community.

Write a list of the core values and traditional principles of socialist theory and ensure that you can define each of them fully and precisely.

Now test yourself

Tested

1 Distinguish between fundamentalist and revisionist socialism.
2 In what sense do socialists have a positive view of human nature?
3 Why have socialists favoured cooperation over competition?
4 Give three reasons why socialists favour social equality.

Answers on p. 76

Revolutionary socialism

Revolutionary socialists seek **communism**: the complete abolition of the capitalist economy and state, and the achievement of a wholly egalitarian society based upon common ownership.

However, revolutionary socialists disagree upon the details of how to get there. There are two main schools of revolutionary socialism:

- Utopian or 'ethical' socialism.
- Marxism or 'scientific' socialism.

Communism — an economic system based on common ownership of wealth and social equality.

Utopian socialism

Revised

A utopia is any ideal society, system or way of life. **Utopianism** — devised by Sir Thomas More in his *Utopia* (1516) — is a form of theorising about a perfect but non-existent society, usually devised to highlight and criticise the perceived evils of present-day society.

- The positive concept of utopianism implies a highly optimistic view of human nature as perfectible — e.g. William Godwin's assertion that 'Perfectibility is the most unequivocal characteristic of the human species' — and a vision of utopia that is believed to be attainable.
- Anarchist and socialist writers, with their view of human nature as sociable and gregarious, are most often utopian.
- There is no common perception of utopia; different philosophies envisage different 'ideals' and, even within a philosophy such as utopian socialism, many different utopias have been devised by different thinkers.
- The negative concept of utopianism implies an over-optimistic view of human nature and an idealistic, moralistic style of theorising which envisages an unattainable fantasy.

Utopianism — a form of theorising which embraces the vision of a perfect alternative society. 'Utopianism' now widely suggests an over-idealised view of human nature and a blueprint of an idealised future society, perhaps without adequate means of achieving that vision of utopia.

Examiner's tip

'Utopianism' has both a positive and a negative interpretation. When answering questions about how utopian a theory is, always address both interpretations.

Utopian socialists advanced a moral critique of capitalism as based on exploitation, avarice and injustice. Each tried to conceive or build a utopia based upon socialist principles of cooperation and social justice which would counter the evils of industrial capitalism and allow humans to flourish as rational and fulfilled beings. Three of the most well-known utopian socialists were:

- Robert Owen (1771–1858) British
- Charles Fourier (1772–1837) French
- Etienne Cabet (1788–1858) American

Now test yourself

Tested ☐

5 Who devised the concept of 'utopia'?

6 What is a 'utopia'?

7 Why are utopian socialists so called?

8 Name one nineteenth-century utopian socialist.

Answers on p. 76

Marxism

Revised ☐

- Marxism is a materialist theory: i.e. it sees economic factors as primary. Engels applied the label 'dialectical materialism' to Marx's theory of historical progress through economic conflict.

- Marxism perceives human history as a series of economic stages of society, most of which contain two main classes.

- In the capitalist stage, the bourgeoisie (ruling class) take the surplus value created by the proletariat (workers), as it is the only possible source of profit (since only labour creates new value). This constitutes exploitation, which generates class conflict.

- This, combined with economic crises and recessions, will eventually make the workers aware of the fact that the capitalist system is only serving the interests of the minority ruling class; and the workers will rise up in revolution to overthrow capitalism and create a transitional phase of 'dictatorship' — class rule — by the proletariat.

- When all industry is collectively owned, classes will have been abolished and communism will have been achieved.

- The state is merely the political agent of the economic ruling class in every class stage of human society. Therefore, when classes have been abolished, the (proletarian) state will simply 'wither away'.

- This analysis of human progress through economic conflict, says Marx, is not wishful thinking but 'scientific determinism', i.e. it is inevitable.

Typical mistake

Marxist theory is very different from 'communist' practice in the USSR and Eastern Europe in the twentieth century but students often wrongly confuse or conflate them. For example, by 'dictatorship', Marx meant rule by one class, *not* rule by an autocrat like Stalin.

Now test yourself

Tested ☐

9 What is meant by saying that Marxism is a materialist theory?

10 Name the two main classes in capitalism.

11 Why is exploitation inevitable in capitalism?

12 What did Marx mean by 'dictatorship of the proletariat'?

13 Why, according to Marx, will the state ultimately and inevitably disappear?

Answers on p. 76

Utopian versus scientific socialism

Table 3.1 Utopian versus scientific socialism

Utopian socialism	Scientific socialism
Emotive and moralistic	Objective and empirical
Capitalism is 'evil'	Capitalism is a necessary economic stage
Focus on ends	Focus on means
Wishful thinking	Determinist and predictive

However, Marxism itself may be perceived by critics — such as conservatives and liberals — as 'utopian' in anticipating a near-perfect future society and being over-optimistic about human nature and about the possibilities for social change.

Evolutionary socialism

Evolutionary socialists have accepted the liberal framework of pluralist, parliamentary democracy, constitutionalism and consent. Their goals are usually more limited and moderate than those of the revolutionary communists; they very rarely seek the wholesale abolition of classes, and none of them seeks the disappearance of the state.

> **Examiner's tip**
>
> The 'evolutionary road', the 'parliamentary road' and 'gradualism' all mean the same thing: the peaceful, ballot-box route to socialism rather than mass working-class revolution.

The inevitability of gradualism

By the turn of the twentieth century, many evolutionary socialists had come to see the parliamentary road as not only desirable, but inevitable, for the following reasons:

- The working class had been given the right to vote.
- The working class were by far the majority class.
- They would naturally vote for socialist parties which would act in their best class interests.
- Socialist parties would, therefore, regularly win electoral success and implement socialist policies.
- Socialism via the ballot box was thus inevitable, rendering revolution redundant.

> **Typical mistake**
>
> 'Gradualism' does not mean that the process of change is necessarily slow; it refers to the use of the parliamentary road.

Hence British Labour Party founder Sidney Webb's famous use of the phrase 'the inevitability of gradualism'.

> **Now test yourself**   Tested
>
> 14 What is meant by 'evolutionary socialism'?
> 15 How do revolutionary and evolutionary socialists differ in their attitude to the state?
> 16 Who spoke of 'the inevitability of gradualism', and why?
>
> Answers on pp. 76–77

Fundamentalist versus revisionist socialism

Revised

Fundamentalist socialism rejects capitalism entirely and seeks to abolish and replace capitalism. It usually attributes the flaws of capitalism to private property for private profit, and seeks to establish socialism in the form of common ownership and very substantial equality of outcome. The Marxist or communist tradition is the clearest example of fundamentalist socialism. However, some fundamentalists pursue their goals by the parliamentary road — i.e. it is possible to be 'fundamentalist democrats' in the parliamentary sense. Eurocommunists (the post-war Western European communist parties) and early Fabians such as the Webbs were parliamentary socialists who were, nevertheless, fundamentalist in their goals.

Revisionist socialism, by contrast, seeks to reform or tame capitalism rather than abolish it. It practises an accommodationist strategy — in a sense, it seeks to reconcile socialism with capitalism. It seeks social justice in the sense of narrowing the economic and social inequalities (to varying degrees) within capitalism through welfare and redistribution. Social democracy is the most obvious example of revisionist socialism. Revisionists are invariably parliamentary, not revolutionary, socialists.

The distinction between the two therefore lies in their different goals and hence different definitions of 'socialism'. Their means — revolution or evolution — may or may not be the same.

> **Typical mistake**
>
> 'Fundamentalism' versus 'revisionism' does not mean 'revolutionary' versus 'parliamentary'.

> **Examiner's tip**
>
> When essays ask about the goals of socialism — for example, the extent to which they support equality of outcome or common ownership of wealth — good essay introductions will define 'fundamentalism' versus 'revisionism' as the structural base for the rest of the essay.

Main sub-strands within evolutionary socialism

Revised

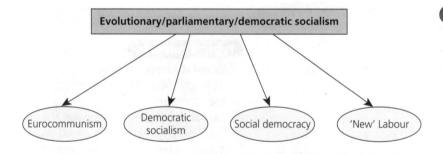

Figure 3.1 The main sub-strands of evolutionary/parliamentary/democratic socialism

> **Examiner's tip**
>
> 'Democratic socialism' has two meanings: (i) broadly, all forms of parliamentary socialism; (ii) narrowly, radical left-wing 'old' Labour parliamentary socialism. If you are required to use and define this concept, always give both the broad and the narrow definitions. If an exam question includes this concept, consider the broad definition first.

The rise of evolutionary socialism

Revised

Reasons for the rise of evolutionary (parliamentary) socialism include:

- Extension of the franchise (the vote) in the late nineteenth and early twentieth centuries, first to the middle classes and then, most importantly, to the working class.
- Christian Methodism, which rejected the violence likely to accompany revolution.
- Increasingly strong capitalist states capable of preventing revolutionary social change.

> **Now test yourself**
>
> 17 List three sub-strands of parliamentary socialism.
>
> 18 List three reasons why socialists adopted the parliamentary road rather than the revolutionary road.
>
> **Answers on p. 77**
>
> Tested

Eurocommunism

Revised

'Eurocommunism' was the label applied to the Western communist parties (French, Italian, Spanish, British etc.) from the 1970s to the 1990s, when they abandoned revolutionary Marxism (for the reasons outlined above) and pursued a parliamentary road to communism. With the collapse of orthodox communism in Eastern Europe and the fall of the Berlin Wall in 1989, this theory was abandoned, and Western Eurocommunism is now just a historical curiosity, largely ignored.

> **Typical mistake**
>
> Some students make the mistake of equating Eurocommunism with twentieth-century, Eastern European, one-party communism.

Democratic socialism

Revised

- Early evolutionary socialists such as Sidney Webb (1859–1947) remained 'fundamentalist' in their goals: that is, they still sought the complete overthrow of capitalism, but via the ballot box rather than by revolution. Sidney Webb wrote the original Clause 4 of the UK Labour Party constitution (1918) which asserted the goal of common ownership.
- Equality of ownership meant extensive state nationalisation rather than direct takeover of the factories by the workers.
- Equality of outcome meant high taxation by the state of the most wealthy and extensive state welfare for the less well-off.
- Crucially, therefore, evolutionary socialists revised their analysis of the state. Rather than seeing it as an irredeemable tool of the ruling class, they came to see it as a potential vehicle for progressive socialist advancement and reform.

> **Typical mistake**
>
> Students sometimes wrongly label democratic socialism as revisionist because it is a parliamentary form of socialism; this indicates a misunderstanding of the term 'revisionist'.

Why and how do socialists promote collectivism?

Revised

Why do socialists promote collectivism?

- Collectivism advances a belief in the community, social group or collective body, emphasising the social character of humankind and its capacity for collective action.
- Socialists stress altruistic humans' ability and willingness to work together cooperatively for the common good. They believe that selfish individualism is not innate but is a result of social conditioning, and that society functions best, in both practical and ethical terms, when people act collectively and harmoniously.
- Generally, socialists promote collective action in pursuit of their goals of equality, social justice, community, harmony and democracy, because of their optimistic view of human nature.

How do socialists promote collectivism? By a variety of means:

- Some utopian socialists such as Fourier and Owen set up experimental communes.
- Revolutionary socialists promote it via mass working-class uprising, collective ownership of the means of production and the abolition or disappearance of the state in favour of forms of direct democracy.
- Evolutionary socialists promote it via state nationalisation, redistribution through progressive taxation, extensive welfarism and trade union organisation, rights and activities.

> **Typical mistake**
>
> When students are answering a 'Why and how...' short question, they sometimes answer the 'why' part and then forget to answer the 'how' part. Remember that two-part questions require two-part answers.

> **Now test yourself**
>
> 19 Define 'Eurocommunism'.
> 20 What was Clause 4?
> 21 Suggest three ways in which socialists promote collectivism.
>
> Answers on p. 77
>
> Tested

Reasons for post-war revisionism

Socialism moved to the right after the Second World War for several reasons:

- Nationalism and patriotism were engendered by two world wars.
- The Cold War generated profound ideological hostility in the West towards any form of radical socialism.
- The post-war economic boom meant that capitalism appeared to be delivering the goods in terms of increasing living standards and welfare for the working class.
- These economies were also changing shape: traditional 'blue-collar' industries were declining and the 'white-collar' service sector was growing. The traditional working class was diminishing in number, and the middle classes were increasing in number.
- Parliamentary socialist policies such as state nationalisation were often seen as inefficient, bureaucratic, impersonal and restrictive of freedom, choice and personal autonomy.
- Socialisation — especially by an increasingly influential, capitalist, mass media.

All of these factors meant that the popularity of radical socialist ideas declined markedly. Instead, 'revisionist' social democracy emerged.

Social democracy

Post-war socialist parties, therefore, abandoned 'fundamentalism' for 'revisionism': they no longer sought to abolish capitalism but merely to reform it, seeking an accommodation between the economic efficiency of market capitalism and the ethical appeal of state socialism.

This produced '**social democracy**': a mixed economy which combined private and state ownership, with moderate welfare and a more liberal emphasis on equality of opportunity rather than the far-reaching socialist goal of equality of outcome.

> **Social democracy** — a revisionist form of parliamentary socialism which has accommodated to capitalism and favours a Keynesian mixed economy.

Now test yourself

Tested

22 Define 'revisionism'.
23 Give three reasons for the post-war revisionist shift in socialist thought.

Answers on p. 77

Divisions within 'old' Labour

Table 3.2 Divisions within 'old' Labour

Democratic socialism	Social democracy
Radical	Reformist
More 'left wing'	More 'right wing'
Mainly collective economy	Mainly private economy
Equality	Freedom and fairness
Extensive welfare state	Extended welfare state
Anti-private health/education	Pro-choice
Abolish Lords	Reform Lords
Anti-EU	Pro-EU
Unilateral nuclear disarmament	Multilateral disarmament
More internationalist	More nationalist
More principled	More pragmatic
More emphasis on goals	More emphasis on means

Typical mistake

Students often confuse 'democratic socialism' and 'social democracy'. Here is one way of remembering the difference between them: 'democratic *socialism*' is genuinely socialist, whereas '*social* democracy' is merely social, i.e. collectivist but not wholly anti-capitalist.

Revision activity

List five differences between democratic socialism and social democracy to produce two contrasting tables.

Reasons for 1990s' neo-revisionism

A further shift to the right within socialist thought occurred in the 1990s, for the following reasons:

- The continuing shrinkage of the working class and growth of the middle class.
- Repeated election defeats — for example, four successive general election defeats of the British Labour Party 1979–97.
- The almost irreversible impact of New Right conservative ideology and policies since the 1970s.
- The collapse of communism in 1989 which suggested to some that socialism itself was dead.
- Economic globalisation which meant that international capitalism was increasingly entrenched and pervasive.

All these factors led to the emergence of the neo-revisionist 'third way'.

The 'third way'

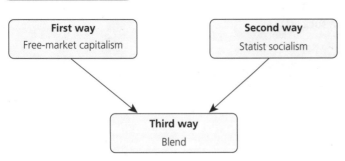

Figure 3.2 Origins of the 'third way'

- The '**third way**' was a slogan which sought to locate a yet more right-wing position, between free-market capitalism and state socialism.
- The slogan and concept was originally devised by the Italian fascist leader Benito Mussolini in the 1930s, implicitly developed in post-war social democracy and explicitly adopted in the 1990s by 'neo-revisionist' movements such as US Clinton's Democrats and UK Blair's 'New' Labour.

Third way — a neo-revisionist blend of free market capitalism and state socialism.

Exam practice answers and quick quizzes at **www.therevisionbutton.co.uk/myrevisionnotes**

- It involved concepts such as 'stakeholding' and 'social inclusion' — seeking to involve and provide wider opportunities for more people, including the disadvantaged, within a market-oriented capitalist economy where every individual has both rights and responsibilities.
- It seemed, to critics, a quite incoherent and an opportunistic mix of market capitalism combined with communitarian liberal rights and responsibilities, with a dose of social authoritarianism thrown in.
- Thus parliamentary socialism has slid inexorably to the right over the twentieth century, abandoning most of its core values and principles along the way.

Revision activities

- Write a list of five specific sub-strands of socialist thought, with a 5–10-line summary description of each.
- Write a list of the quotations contained in this chapter, with names for all of them, and decide how you would use each one in exam answers.

Predominant schools of thought within the British Labour Party since 1900

| 1900–1950s Democratic socialist radicalism | → | 1950s–1990s Social democratic reform | → | 1990s onwards 'New' Labour/'third way' |

Figure 3.3 Changes in parliamentary socialism since 1900

Examiner's tip

Figure 3.3, from left to right, provides a useful framework for essay questions which ask about the changing nature of parliamentary socialism over the last century.

Now test yourself

Tested

24 List three differences between democratic socialism and social democracy.
25 Give two reasons for the neo-revisionist shift to the 'third way'.
26 Define the 'third way'.

Answers on p. 77

Exam practice

A Short-answer questions

1 Why did Marx believe that capitalism was doomed to collapse?
2 Distinguish between fundamentalist and revisionist socialism.
3 Why have socialists favoured cooperation over competition?

B Essay questions

4 To what extent have socialists been committed to equality of outcome?
5 To what extent have socialists disagreed about the means of achieving socialism?
6 'Communism and social democracy offer starkly different models of socialism.' Discuss.

Answers and quick quiz 3 online

Online

Examiner's summary

✔ Some exam questions are exclusively about Marxist theory, in which case there is rarely any need to refer to the wider schools of socialist thought.

✔ Short questions often ask for definitions and explanations of core socialist concepts and doctrines, such as collectivism and equality.

✔ Short questions sometimes ask about the difference between fundamentalist and revisionist socialism; do not confuse this with the differences between revolutionary and evolutionary socialism.

✔ Many essay questions on socialism require comparisons and contrasts across the diverse schools of socialist thought, sometimes on a core issue such as the extent of support for common ownership or rejection of private property.

✔ Essay questions sometimes ask about the extent and reasons for socialism's retreat from its traditional principles; answers should be structured chronologically, starting with revolutionary socialism and ending with the 'third way'.

4 Anarchism

Anarchism is a philosophy which rejects all forms of coercion, especially state and government. The term derives from the ancient Greek meaning, literally 'no rule', and is often used negatively to imply chaos and disorder. The nineteenth-century anarchist Pierre-Joseph Proudhon (1809–65) was the first to announce proudly, in 1840, 'I am an anarchist' — as an advocate of direct self-government, personal freedom and rejection of all forms of power.

> **Anarchism** — a broad-ranging philosophy which rejects all forms of coercion and most forms of authority, especially state and government.

Core principles of anarchism

Core principles — Revised

- All anarchists reject state and government. (They point out that, until some six thousand years ago, all humans lived in stateless societies and, therefore, could readily do so again.)
- They all have a highly optimistic view of human nature. One of the earliest anarchistic thinkers, William Godwin (1793), went so far as to say that 'Perfectibility is the most unequivocal characteristic of the human species'. Where humans are bad, say anarchists, this is due to the corrupting influence of state power and exploitation — hence it is a product of nurture, not nature.
- They all, therefore, share the common philosophical goal of freedom as a primary objective.
- They all reject orthodox forms of representative democracy, dismissing them as a sham and a facade where voters surrender their personal **autonomy** and thus collude in their own oppression.
- Finally, since they all seek a fundamental transformation of society, they are all revolutionary.

> **Examiner's tip**
> Check the handy AFFORD mnemonic below!
> **A**narchism
> **F**aith in human nature
> **F**reedom as a primary goal
> **O**pposition to all forms of coercive power, especially state and government
> **R**evolutionary transformation of existing society
> **D**irect democracy

> **Autonomy** — literally, self-government: the ability to control one's own personal destiny, free from external control or coercion.

> **Typical mistake**
> Do not employ the term 'anarchy' to mean chaos and disorder as some mainstream politicians and media do; anarchists strongly believe that stateless human societies are the best recipe for spontaneous order and harmony.

> **Typical mistake**
> Because anarchists reject representative democracy, students sometimes wrongly assert that anarchism is anti-democratic. However, anarchism very strongly favours direct democracy.

The state is unnecessary — Revised

Why do anarchists believe that the state is unnecessary?

- Anarchists' optimistic views of human nature lead them to conclude that humans do not need a state to maintain social order and harmony.

Exam practice answers and quick quizzes at **www.therevisionbutton.co.uk/myrevisionnotes**

- Indeed, the state, as an inherently coercive power body, will pervert peoples' capacity for spontaneous social order and harmony.

The state is undesirable

Why do anarchists believe that the state is undesirable?

- The state is a sovereign power body and is therefore, by definition, untameable. (Anarchists think that liberals are deluding themselves on this point.)
- The state is compulsory — we did not opt to live under it and we cannot opt out of it. (Anarchists think that the liberal belief in some sort of 'social contract' between individuals and the state is, again, delusional.)
- The state is coercive — it can impose laws and punishments upon individuals, sometimes even the death penalty.
- The state is exploitative — its taxation powers amount to legalised theft.
- The state is destructive — it wages devastating wars against other states.

Revision activity

Complete the mnemonic below:

A
F
F
O
R
D

Now test yourself

Tested

1 What was the original Greek meaning of 'anarchy'?
2 List four doctrines which are common to all anarchists.
3 Give one name and quotation which illustrates anarchist optimism about human nature.
4 Why do anarchists reject representative democracy?
5 Give three reasons why anarchists think that the state is undesirable.

Answers on p. 77

Examiner's tip

Answers to exam questions on why anarchists believe that the state is unnecessary should focus on their optimistic views of human nature. Answers to exam questions on why anarchists believe that the state is undesirable should focus on the intrinsic nature of the state itself as a coercive power body.

Typical mistake

Students sometimes wrongly confuse or conflate two question themes: the view of the state as unnecessary (due to anarchists' optimistic view of human nature) and the view of the state as undesirable (because anarchists see the state as intrinsically coercive).

Objection to constitutionalism and consent

Why do anarchists object to constitutionalism and consent?

- Constitutionalism is the exercise or advocacy of a set of rules and principles which limit the power of state and government. Consent is the concept that the right to govern derives from the explicit agreement of the governed, usually through the mechanism of free and fair elections. Both of these concepts are central to liberal theory.

- Anarchists object to them because both principles promise to limit and legitimise the power of the state, but anarchists believe that such power is absolute, evil and untameable. This belief derives from the idea of the absolutely corrupting nature of power and the premise that the state as a sovereign power body is intrinsically coercive, exploitative and destructive.

- Most importantly, both principles recruit people into colluding with their own oppression by concealing the reality of state power. Constitutionalism perpetuates the myths of limited government and respect for the 'rule of law' — although, from an anarchist viewpoint, all law negates liberty. Consent perpetuates the myths of legitimate government authority, public accountability and rule in the public interest — although, from an anarchist viewpoint, we never truly consented to live under the power of a state and can never opt out of it.

Typical mistake

It is not sufficient to say, as many students do, that these principles are associated with state authority, and anarchists are anti-statist and therefore against all associated principles.

Examiner's tip

A good exam answer should always, first, define and not simply assume the key title concepts.

Now test yourself

Tested

6　Why do anarchists object to constitutionalism?

7　Why do anarchists object to consent?

Answers on p. 77

Diverse theories of anarchism

The two major strands ━━━━━━━━━━━━━━━━━━━━━━━━━━━━━━ Revised

There are two major strands to anarchist thought (with many sub-strands): collectivist — **ultra-socialism**, and individualist — **ultra-liberalism**.

- **Ultra-socialists** are left-wing, revolutionary, **utopian** collectivists who have strong faith in human goodness and seek various forms of egalitarian society.

- **Ultra-liberals**, on the other hand, are individualists who often advocate undiluted free-market economics — e.g. 'anarcho-capitalists'. This is, arguably, nineteenth-century liberalism pushed to its logical extreme.

Utopianism — a form of theorising which envisages a perfect, imaginary society, usually devised as an ethical critique of the perceived ills of present society.

Within these broad categories there are several sub-strands of anarchism, as depicted in the diagram below.

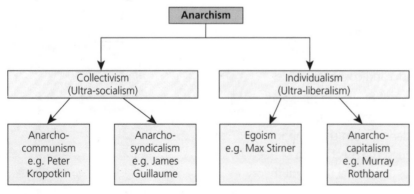

Figure 4.1 Strands of thought within anarchism

Collectivist anarchism

Anarcho-communism — advocacy of small, egalitarian and directly democratic communes, based on common economic ownership, with no state.

Anarcho-syndicalism — a form of revolutionary trade unionism which, via a general strike, would establish workers' syndicates, with no state.

Anarcho-capitalism — advocacy of a completely *laissez-faire*, private enterprise economy, with no state.

Egoism — the belief that the rational individual is at the centre of his or her moral universe, with absolute personal autonomy and no need of a state or any other source of control or authority.

Collectivism
Revised

Collectivism is the belief that cooperative social action is both more ethical and more efficient than is selfish individualism. It is based on the belief that humans are social creatures with an innate tendency towards altruistic, cooperative and social behaviour. The logic of this stance is that a peaceful and harmonious society can be achieved naturally and spontaneously through cooperation between social groups, without the need for a coercive state above them.

Collectivism therefore leads quite logically to anarchist beliefs with their rejection of the state and other forms of coercive power. The link is found in the ideas and theories of collectivist anarchism, which has a highly optimistic view of human nature as social, gregarious and ultimately perfectible. It therefore envisages a peaceful and harmonious society functioning through cooperative social groups with no coercive state and government over them — e.g. Kropotkin's anarcho-communism. There are many diverse theories of collectivist anarchism, but they all share the same basic optimism about human nature.

Anarcho-communism
Revised

Anarcho-communists envisage a radically decentralised society of small, egalitarian and self-governing communes which operate and interrelate on the basis of cooperation and communitarianism.

Anarcho-syndicalism
Revised

Anarcho-syndicalists are more focused upon the collective ownership of industry and the economy by revolutionary workers' syndicates representing the various sectors of the economy (manufacturing, construction, agriculture and so on) but without a coercive workers' state at the top.

Individualist anarchism

Individualism Revised

Individualism asserts the primacy of the rights and freedoms of every individual above any group, society or state. This logically implies the need to do away with the state because it is a sovereign and coercive power entity which inevitably constrains individual freedoms.

Individualism views human nature as rational and self-interested, which also logically implies that individuals do not need a state to determine their own best interests, but can do it themselves.

> **Typical mistake**
>
> It is incorrect and overly simplistic to think that 'collectivism' and 'individualism' are exact opposites.

Anarcho-capitalism Revised

One form of individualist anarchism, **anarcho-capitalism**, envisages an absolutely unfettered free market without any punitive or oppressive state taxation, regulation and interference. Other individualists support libertarian visions based upon non-exploitative market interaction (time stores).

Egoism Revised

Max Stirner's **egoism** is most starkly individualist: each person is the centre of his or her own moral universe in a stateless society where the rationalism of human beings will be the best guarantee of social order.

> **Examiner's tip**
>
> These four sub-strands of anarchist thought — anarcho-communism, anarcho-syndicalism, anarcho-capitalism and egoism, in this order, — provide a useful typology and structure for many essays on anarchism.

> **Typical mistake**
>
> Students are sometimes too sweeping and simplistic when describing anarchist views of human nature; it is important to distinguish between the collectivist and the individualist views.

> **Revision activity**
>
> Create four cue cards, one for each main sub-strand of anarchist thought, describing the main doctrines, principles, aims and methods of each.

Other visions of the stateless society

Proudhon Revised

Between these clear constructs, the visions of people like Proudhon and Tucker are less starkly collectivist or individualist. Proudhon's '**mutualist**' vision of libertarian socialism, for example, allows for small-scale property ownership and mutual cooperation.

In sum, there are probably almost as many visions of a stateless society as there are anarchist visionaries — as befits the philosophy itself.

> **Mutualism** — Pierre-Joseph Proudhon's theory of fair and equitable bargaining, trade and exchange without exploitation or profiteering — somewhere between collectivism and individualism.

Answers on p. 77

Now test yourself

Tested

8 Distinguish between the collectivist anarchist and the individualist anarchist views of human nature.

9 List the four sub-strands of anarchism.

10 Why are anarchists often labelled 'utopian'?

11 Summarise the goals of anarcho-communism.

12 Name two left-wing anarchists.

13 Who devised the theory of 'egoism'?

14 Name one anarcho-capitalist.

Revision activities

● From memory, draw a diagram depicting the two major strands of anarchist thought and their four sub-strands.

● Explain in what ways (a) individualist anarchism is 'right wing' and (b) collectivist anarchism is 'left wing'.

Anarchism versus Marxism

Similarities and differences

Revised

There are clear similarities between the goals and end visions of collectivist anarchism and Marxism.

However, anarchists and Marxists differ most obviously on their view of the state. Marxism is a materialist theory which focuses primarily on the economic infrastructure and perceives human progress resulting from economic conflict. Marxism believes that the state is mere 'superstructure' — essentially a reflection of the class system and the political agent of the economic ruling class rather than being oppressive in its own right. For Marxism, society cannot be transformed simply by smashing the mirror. The proletariat must first overthrow the bourgeoisie in a class revolution and they must then establish a temporary workers' state — a proletarian dictatorship — to guard against counter-revolution. This proletarian state is justifiable and progressive as a transitional phase, but it will wither away as a consequence of the abolition of classes.

Typical mistake

Do not overstate Marxism's attachment to the state; the theory endorses only a temporary and transitional state.

For anarchists, on the other hand, the state is the primary target of attack. For them, it is a concentrated form of evil in itself, given the tendency of power to corrupt absolutely. States, by this view, exercise sovereign, compulsory, coercive, exploitative, oppressive and destructive authority. Humans are sufficiently altruistic or rational to govern and organise themselves harmoniously.

Marxists, who do share the anarchist goal of the stateless society, also point out that, while anarchists are very good at condemning the state, they are not very good at *explaining* the state. If human nature is potentially so good and the state is so intrinsically evil, oppressive and corrupting, how and why did it come into being in the first place, why is it so persistent and pervasive, and why do most people not see through its consensual facade it and reject it more readily?

Finally, whilst collectivist schools of anarchism are forms of ultra-socialism with similar goals to those of Marxism, individualist schools of anarchism — especially anarcho-capitalism — are forms of ultra-liberalism whose hostility to the state derives from a belief in the very free-market capitalism which spawned Marxism as its antithesis.

Table 4.1 Marxism versus anarchism

Marxism	Anarchism
Materialist theory	Political theory
Scientific socialism	Utopian socialism
State is mere superstructure	State is primary target
Explains state	Condemns state
Endorses proletarian state	Rejects any state
State will wither away	State must be overthrown

Examiner's tip

When comparing and contrasting anarchism and Marxism, start by explaining the similarities and then address the differences, especially between individualist anarchism and Marxism.

Revision activity

Devise a table listing four main differences between collectivist anarchism and Marxism.

Anarchism versus liberalism

Extreme form of liberalism

Revised

All anarchists, like all liberals, perceive individual freedom as a primary doctrine, because they have faith in human nature and humans' capacity to exercise freedom responsibly.

Individualist anarchism is an extreme form of liberalism — ultra-liberalism — in the sense that it was born out of classical liberal theory, is based on the idea of the sovereign individual and favours private property and (usually) free-market economics. It takes to its logical extreme the early liberal view that the state is a 'realm of coercion', and also Mill's dictum 'Over himself, over his own body and mind, the individual is sovereign'. It shares the liberal view of human nature as rational and self-striving, and therefore as deserving of freedom from any coercion and control, especially from state and government. Anarcho-capitalism, most obviously, is an extension of classical *laissez-faire* liberalism. Max Stirner's theory of egoism takes to its logical conclusion the liberal belief that individuals should be primarily concerned with their own interests and welfare, should be the centre of their own moral universe and should have complete moral autonomy.

However, all anarchists believe that humans cannot have freedom with a state, whereas all liberals believe that humans cannot have freedom without a state. Anarchists see the state as irredeemably evil, oppressive and corrupting, whereas liberals perceive that the state can act to protect and even enhance individuals' freedom. Even classical liberals saw the state as a 'necessary evil' to safeguard law and order; and modern liberals favour an interventionist state to enhance positive freedom. Hence all anarchists are revolutionary, whereas liberals are, at most, reformist. Liberals would also very largely reject the violent tactics employed by some anarchists.

Finally, whilst individualist schools of anarchism are forms of ultra-liberalism, collectivist schools of anarchism are forms of ultra-socialism born out of opposition to the classical liberal economics which most individualists espouse.

Examiner's tip

When exam questions ask about comparisons and contrasts between anarchism and liberalism, point out that individualist anarchists and liberals share a common view of human nature as rational and self-interested, but they draw different conclusions from it about the need for a state.

Table 4.2 Liberalism versus anarchism

Liberalism	Anarchism
State is necessary evil (classical)	State is unnecessary evil
State aids positive freedom (modern)	State negates freedom
Favours constitutionalism and consent	Believes both are sham
'Rule of law' protects liberty	All law infringes liberty
Reformist	Revolutionary

> **Typical mistake**
>
> It is wrong to overstate liberalism's attachment to the state; all liberals believe the state to be evil, yet necessary.

Are anarchists just extreme liberals?

Revised

- The question is posed because the roots of some anarchist thinking lie in classical liberalism; and because anarchists and liberals share a belief in human rationality and a fundamental desire for freedom. However, anarchism is a very broad-ranging and revolutionary philosophy which goes well beyond even 'extreme' liberalism.

- Liberalism in the nineteenth century favoured *laissez-faire* libertarianism and negative freedom. Individualist anarchists apparently took this philosophy to its logical conclusion and advocated various forms of 'ultra-liberalism', whether individualist amoralism or anarcho-capitalism.

- However, even classical liberals always advocated a 'nightwatchman state' to ensure order. Modern liberals have become more pro-state with the advocacy of positive freedom. No liberal, however extreme, would advocate the complete abolition of state and government. Anarchists and liberals thus have qualitatively different views about freedom and the role of the state in protecting or threatening it.

- Also, liberals are reformist rather than revolutionary; and they would reject many of the tactics employed by violent anarchists.

- Moreover, there is a major school of collectivist anarchism which arose out of opposition to classical free-market liberalism itself.

- Anarchists are not, therefore, just extreme liberals. Anarchists and liberals have different concepts of freedom deriving from different views of the state; and anarchism is a much more diverse, revolutionary and anti-constitutional theory than is liberalism of any sort.

> **Examiner's tip**
>
> When an exam question takes the form 'Is X just/merely/only/simply/solely Y?', the answer is invariably 'No' because the question is too absolute.

> **Revision activity**
>
> Devise a table listing four main differences between individualist anarchism and liberalism.

Now test yourself

Tested

15 List three similarities and three differences between anarchism and Marxism.

16 List three similarities and three differences between anarchism and liberalism.

Answers on pp. 77–78

Anarchist strategies and tactics

Range of methods

Revised

The methods of political action and social transition advocated by anarchists are many and varied.

Anarchism was originally — and logically — pacifist (e.g. Proudhon, Kropotkin and the writer Leo Tolstoy). Since anarchists reject coercion in all its forms, and since violence is the ultimate form of coercion, most anarchists naturally reject it.

Some anarchists, however, have turned to violence, either in the form of terrorism (e.g. Bakunin) or the potentially violent general strike (Guillaume) due to frustration at their lack of success, a belief in the nihilistic virtue of destruction, the need to counter a violent state or simply the desire to expose the inherently violent nature of the state by provoking it. This tactical divide between pacifist and violent anarchism is found mainly within the left-wing, collectivist strand of the philosophy.

Thus the range of methods employed by anarchists includes: peaceful education and persuasion; propaganda; mass, passive resistance to the state; non-payment of taxes; boycotts of key institutions, products and companies; strikes and other forms of industrial action; meetings, marches and demonstrations; extending market institutions and structures; committing 'acts of senseless beauty' such as painting the lampposts green; civil disobedience, i.e. forms of peaceful law-breaking as political protest (associated particularly with the American libertarian Henry Thoreau); riots and insurrection; and acts of violence and terrorism, particularly against politicians, judges and military leaders.

What anarchists philosophically cannot do is participate in mainstream, orthodox, ballot-box and party politics, since that would be subscribing to the politics of the state.

Revision activity

Do an internet search and find three anarchist groups in the UK. What can you find out about their aims and methods?

Revision activity

List ten possible methods employed by anarchists.

Examiner's tip

When exam questions ask about the methods employed by anarchists, remember to think across all the sub-strands and to cite both collectivist and individualist methods.

Typical mistake

It is wrong to overstate anarchists' tendency to use violence and terror; there is, logically, a strong legacy of pacifism within anarchism.

Now test yourself

17 List five methods employed by anarchists.

Answers on p. 78

Tested

Exam practice

A Short-answer questions

1 Why have anarchists viewed the state as evil and oppressive?
2 How do the anarchist and Marxist views of the state differ?
3 Explain the link between anarchism and individualism.

B Essay questions

4 To what extent is anarchism a utopian creed?
5 Is anarchism closer to socialism or to liberalism?
6 'Anarchism is strong on moral principles but weak on political practice.' Discuss

Answers and quick quiz 4 online

Online

Examiner's summary

✔ There are a few common doctrines upon which all anarchists broadly agree, but there are major differences across the sub-strands.

✔ The diverse schools of anarchist thought originate from socialist and liberal theories and span the left and right wing.

✔ Anarchists strongly believe that the state is an unnecessary evil, partly because of their optimistic views on human nature and partly because of the intrinsic role and nature of the state itself.

✔ Collectivist anarchists and Marxists share similar goals, but anarchists disagree with the Marxist view that the state is merely a political agent of the ruling class which will 'wither away' when classes are abolished; for anarchists, the state must be directly targeted and smashed.

✔ Individualist views share the liberal view of human nature and desire for freedom, but they believe that liberal ideas about limiting the power of state and government are self-deluding myths.

✔ Anarchists employ a wide range of strategies and tactics — collectivist and individualist, legal and illegal, peaceful and violent — but they do not subscribe to the politics of state by participating in mainstream party politics and elections.

Table 5.1 Nationalism versus racialism

Nationalism	Racialism
Culture	Biology
No necessary assertion of hierarchy	Hierarchy
Territorial claims	No necessary territorial claims
Left, centre or right wing	Right wing
Rational or irrational	Irrational

Nationalism

A sense of common cultural identity   Revised

Nationalism is a sense of common cultural identity which may be based upon a range of factors such as language, religion, race, history or territory. A nationalist movement usually seeks to defend or to establish a **nation-state**, i.e. a sovereign political territory which houses a community of people who feel themselves to be a cohesive nation.

> **Nation-state** — a sovereign political territory housing a homogeneous cultural community.

Examples:

- Language-based: Plaid Cymru (Welsh nationalists) and ETA (Basque nationalists).
- Religion-based: IRA (Irish republican nationalists) and Palestinians.
- Race-based: Rastafarianism and the Nation of Islam.

Almost all nationalist movements have, or cultivate, a sense of cultural history and tradition; and almost all nationalist movements claim a specific territory as a homeland.

> **Typical mistake**
>
> Students often wrongly define a 'nation' as a common cultural group sharing the same territory. Bear in mind that the people of a nation need not all live in one place; the Scots and Irish, for example, are widely dispersed around the world.

- Nationalism is often perceived as a single doctrine which can attach itself to almost any wider political ideology such as liberalism, conservatism, fascism and even socialism — hence it is one of the most flexible of all modern political tenets.
- National identity has at least three dimensions: cultural, political and psychological.
- The concept originated in late eighteenth-century Europe, with the French Revolution and industrialisation.
- Cultural nationalism differs from political nationalism; for example, the former is more exclusive and the latter more inclusive (see below).
- Many writers regard **nations** as 'invented traditions' or 'imagined communities' — that is, as essentially psychological constructs.
- Many **states**, such as the UK and USA, are multi-national or multicultural.

> **Nation** — a cultural entity; a collection of people with a shared sense of common heritage.
>
> **State** — a sovereign, political power over a given territory.

Now test yourself   Tested ☐

1 Define 'nationalism'.
2 Give three examples of nationalist movements.
3 When did nationalism originate?
4 List three dimensions of national identity.

Answers on p. 78

Nation versus state ———————————————————— Revised ☐

Whereas a state is a sovereign, political power over a given territory — which may be multi-national — a nation (a much more recent concept than the idea of the state) is a cultural entity, a collection of people with a shared sense of common heritage. Nationalism is, therefore, sometimes described as a 'psycho-political construct', because it is essentially subjective — a matter of sentiment and self-identity rather than objective character.

Most states, such as the UK and USA, are multicultural and multi-national (the UK, for example, comprises, at least, the English, Scottish, Welsh and Northern Irish nations). Alternatively, a nation may be landless or dispersed across many states — as were, for example, the Jews before the creation of Israel in 1948. Many nations today are still in search of a state: for example, the Palestinians, Kurds, Chechnyans, Basques and Scots.

The aim of most nationalist movements is to create or maintain a nation-state, where the common cultural group equates with a sovereign political unit. Their methods include unification, e.g. the creation of Germany by merging East and West; secession, i.e. break-away, e.g. Eire (Ireland); irredentism (from the Latin *irredentista*, 'unredeemed'), i.e. movements seeking to redeem a lost territory, such as Spain and Gibraltar; or the replacement of a foreign by an indigenous (domestic) leadership, e.g. Palestine versus Israel.

> **Typical mistake**
>
> The concepts of 'nation' and 'state' are sometimes confused but should not be.

> **Examiner's tip**
>
> If an exam question asks about the differences between 'nation' and 'state', focus on the contrasts and do not digress onto similarities or overlaps.

> **Typical mistake**
>
> It is wrong to assert that all nationalist movements seek statehood, but it is correct to assert that most of them do.

Now test yourself   Tested ☐

5 Distinguish between a 'nation' and a 'state'.
6 Why are the two concepts often confused?
7 Give one example of a multicultural state.
8 Why do most nations seek statehood?

Answers on p. 78

Forms of nationalism (listed chronologically) ————————— Revised ☐

Liberal nationalism

This is the earliest form of nationalism. It is associated with the French Revolution and Enlightenment era. Liberal nationalism regards nations in the same way as liberal theory regards individuals: that is, they are deserving of freedom, autonomy and **self-determination**. It is peaceful, constitutional and reformist. However, since liberalism espouses individualism and

> **National self-determination** — the belief that a cultural community should govern itself within a sovereign state.

universalism, it ultimately looks beyond the nation to embrace a form of internationalism, and to support supranational bodies such as the EU. Liberal forms of nationalism are, therefore, inherently contradictory.

Examples: SNP; Plaid Cymru.

Conservative nationalism

This dates from the nineteenth century onwards. It regards cultural unity, **patriotism** and an emotional attachment to the traditional symbols of the state — such as the flag and the monarchy — as sources of social stability and organic cohesion.

Example: English nationalism, which can range from former Prime Minister John Major's romanticised image of old maids on bicycles, warm beer and cricket on the village green, to skinhead football yobbos in St George T-shirts flaunting **xenophobia**.

> **Patriotism** — literally, love of the fatherland; a psychological attachment to one's nation or country.
> **Xenophobia** — an irrational fear or hatred of foreigners.

Chauvinist nationalism

This is manifested mainly in fascism. It is expansionist, aggressive, militarist and **ethnocentric** — that is, embodying a sense, not only of cultural distinction, but also of inherent cultural superiority, justifying the right to impose control and culture upon other states through war and conquest.

Examples: Bosnian Serbs; Iraq's pan-Arab expansionism under Saddam Hussein.

> **Ethnocentrism** — a sense not only of cultural distinction, but also of inherent cultural superiority.

Anti-colonial nationalism

This appears from the twentieth century onwards. It is found mainly in less developed countries seeking freedom from imperial rule combined with economic modernisation — therefore often linked to socialist/communist ideology and sometimes revolutionary. Since communist theory is internationalist, communist forms of nationalism are inherently contradictory.

Examples: India; Vietnam; Cuba under Castro.

> **Typical mistake**
> Students often understandably but wrongly link 'ethnocentrism' to racialism; remember that it means a sense of cultural, not necessarily biological, superiority.

> **Examiner's tip**
> When describing and explaining socialist nationalism, employ concepts associated with socialism more generally, such as collectivism, egalitarianism and pursuit of social harmony.

> **Revision activity**
> Create four cue cards: one each on liberal nationalism, conservative nationalism, chauvinist nationalism and anti-colonial nationalism. These should describe the key features and give specific examples of each form.

Summary of nationalism   Revised ☐

Table 5.2 Summary of nationalism

Liberal nationalism	Conservative nationalism
Peaceful, constitutional, progressive, reformist, seeking self-determination and popular sovereignty.	Traditional, organic, static, emphasising cultural heritage, social stability and the primacy of state over individual.
Anti-colonial nationalism	**Chauvinist nationalism**
Anti-imperialist, usually in 'third-world' economies, often revolutionary and socialist in character.	Expansionist, militarist, aggressive and ethnocentric, sometimes tending to racism — main example is fascism.

> **Examiner's tip**
> Table 5.2 gives a useful typology for most essays on nationalism.

Liberal and anti-colonial nationalism are broadly seen as progressive and forward-looking, rational, liberating and reformist or revolutionary. Conservative and chauvinist nationalism are broadly seen as static or reactionary, irrational, illiberal or oppressive. Chauvinist nationalism, especially, is seen as inherently expansionist, violent and destructive, inevitably linked to suspicion, hostility and conflict. However, all forms may, arguably, exhibit 'negative' traits to some degree.

In sum, therefore, nationalism can be left wing or right wing, democratic or dictatorial, progressive or reactionary, peaceful or violent. It looks both to the past and (often) to the future. It is not a unified or coherent political phenomenon.

Revision activity

Write a paragraph explaining why liberal nationalists dislike and fear chauvinist nationalism.

Now test yourself

Tested ☐

9 List four main types of nationalism, and give one example of each.
10 Define:
   (a) Patriotism.
   (b) Xenophobia.
   (c) Ethnocentrism.

Answers on p. 78

Quotations on nationalism

Revised ☐

- Nationalism is 'a chameleon ideology.' (Anthony D. Smith)
- Nationalism is 'the most vigorous and pervasive of all political creeds.' (Derek Heater)
- 'Workers of the world, unite! You have nothing to lose but your chains — you have a world to win!' (Karl Marx)

Political nationalism versus cultural nationalism

Revised ☐

Nationalism is a psycho-political sentiment or movement based upon a sense of common culture, identified with traits such as language, religion, race, history and/or territory. It is generally said to have emerged at the time of the French Revolution and is an extremely flexible doctrine; Anthony Smith has described it as a 'chameleon ideology' because it can adapt and attach itself to almost any wider philosophy. Political nationalism is defined by the principle of self-determination, whether expressed in the desire for some measure of autonomy in the form of devolution or federalism, or in the fully developed form of sovereign statehood. This is the most common of the two forms of nationalism. It may be liberal (e.g. the Scottish National Party), communist (e.g. Cuba) or chauvinist, i.e. expansionist and aggressive (e.g. Italian fascism).

Cultural nationalism, on the other hand, is associated with the defence of a nation's cultural heritage — e.g. the Welsh desire to protect and promote their distinctive language — without any strong desire for political autonomy. It places primary emphasis on the regeneration of the nation as a distinctive civilisation, rather than as a discreet political community. Heywood describes it as a 'bottom-up' form of nationalism that draws more on 'popular' rituals, traditions or legends than on elite, or 'higher', culture. Sometimes, however, cultural nationalism may develop into political nationalism: e.g. the Welsh now have their own devolved Assembly and attachment to it seems to be growing.

Revision activity

Look at the following characteristics of various forms of nationalism. In a table format, list in the form of nationalism which most clearly displays these characteristics.

- Expansionist, aggressive and ethnocentric.
- Liberating, modernising and revolutionary.
- Organic, patriotic and traditional.
- Peaceful, constitutional and reformist.

Now test yourself   Tested ☐

11 Who described nationalism as 'a chameleon ideology', and why?
12 Name two political ideologies which are essentially anti-nationalist.
13 Distinguish, with examples, between political nationalism and cultural nationalism.

Answers on p. 78

Racialism

Definition ─────────────────────────────────────── Revised ☐

Racism/racialism is the perception that humans can meaningfully be categorised into ethnic or biological castes, and that these groups can be ranked in a hierarchy which has economic, political, social and/or psychological significance. Racial theories are perceived as 'right wing' because they invariably advocate hierarchy and supremacy.

Examples include:

- South African apartheid: goal — racial separation.
- German Nazism: Aryanism and anti-Semitism; goal — genocide.
- American Black Power movement: anti-white: 'It's just like when you've got coffee that's too black, which means it's too strong. What do you do? You integrate it with cream, you make it weak... It used to wake you up, now it puts you to sleep.' (Malcolm X)

- Racialism is a developed theory of biological difference and hierarchy justifying patterned racial discrimination, separation, exile, extermination or genocide.

Race — a group of people with a shared — or perceived — biological and genetic inheritance.

Racialism — the belief that humans are divided into distinct biological and ethnic castes which can be ranked in a hierarchy and which have economic, political and/or social significance.

- Racialism need not be based on skin colour at all (e.g. Nazi anti-Semitism).

- Racialism has long been used to justify and legitimise economic and political power and control by one group over others.

- There is disagreement about the root causes of racialism. The recurrent political impact and success of racialism is largely due to its emotional simplicity and its inherent trait of blaming others for the economic, social and psychological failures of the self; hence its appeal to the resentful and insecure who feel ignored, excluded or disadvantaged by mainstream politics or wider society.

- Contemporary examples of racialism in Western Europe are usually variants of neo-Nazism — e.g. Marine le Pen's National Front in France and the British National Party. They target any convenient ethnic minority such as Jews, blacks and Asians, but especially immigrants and asylum seekers, blaming them for crime, social unrest and indigenous unemployment (although the UK, for example, currently takes just 1.98% of the world's refugees). They are currently fomenting anti-Islamic sentiment in the West, especially since the September 2001 attacks on America and the invasion of Iraq.

- Racialism highlights a core liberal dilemma: how far to tolerate intolerance.

Now test yourself

Tested ☐

14 Define 'racialism' and give three examples.
15 Suggest three causes of racialism.
16 Explain why racialism highlights a core liberal dilemma.

Answers on p. 78

Distinctions and similarities between nationalism and racialism

Distinctions and similarities ————————————————————— Revised ☐

- Nationalism and racialism are often confused, but they are conceptually distinct. The main distinction centres upon culture versus biology. Racism is, therefore, more exclusive than is nationalism.

- Because racialism invariably asserts a hierarchy, it is deemed a right-wing doctrine. Nationalism is a much more diverse and flexible doctrine which can attach itself to almost any wider ideology.

- The two concepts may, however, overlap in some groups and movements.

- The two terms are confused, or used interchangeably, especially by right-wing nationalists who define nationhood in terms of ethnicity. One example is the British National Party, which defines 'Britishness' more in terms of ethnicity and skin colour than by external cultural symbols and attachments.

Nationalism is much more flexible and adaptable, and therefore more prevalent, than is racialism. However, the two doctrines may overlap, both in theory and in practice.

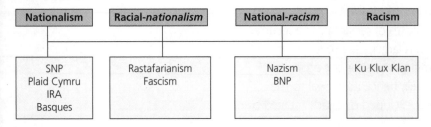

Figure 5.1 Anthony D. Smith's continuum of nationalism and racism, with examples

Distinctions between nations and races

Revised

Nations are cultural entities, whereas races are genetically defined. A nation is a group of people who share a sense of common culture, whether based on language, religion, history and tradition or territorial identity. A **race**, by contrast, is a group of people who are perceived to share a common biological descent and identity and so are regarded as having physical similarities such as skin or hair colour. Just as some argue that nations are essentially imaginary communities, many argue that race is not a meaningful scientific concept — but it clearly often has political or social significance. The two terms are often confused, or used interchangeably, especially by right-wing nationalists who define nationhood in terms of ethnicity — an exclusive perspective usually designed to legitimise hierarchy, separation or other forms of oppression. Conservative nationalism sometimes leans to this perspective, but it is explicit in the ethnic nationalism of Nazism. One contemporary example is the BNP, which defines 'Britishness' more in terms of ethnicity and skin colour than cultural symbols and attachments.

Revision activities

- Explain in what ways (a) conservative nationalism is 'right wing', and (b) anti-colonial nationalism is often 'left wing'.
- List four differences between nationalism and racialism.

Examiner's tip

When exam questions ask why the terms 'nation' and 'race' are sometimes confused, do not make the mistake of confusing or conflating them yourself! Instead, refer to right-wing groups who define the 'nation' in biological terms.

Typical mistake

It is wrong to assume that chauvinist nationalism is always racist; however, it is the form of nationalism which leans most readily to racialism.

Now test yourself

Tested

17 Explain Smith's continuum and give one example of each category.
18 Which UK political party may seek to blur the concepts of 'nation' and 'race'?

Answers on p. 78

Examiner's summary

✔ Nationalism is a subjective concept — a 'psycho-political construct'. It is one of the most flexible political doctrines, with at least three dimensions: cultural, political and psychological.

✔ A common theme of exam short questions is the relationship between the concepts of 'nation' and 'state'.

✔ There are four main types of nationalism: liberal, conservative, chauvinist and anti-colonial. This is a useful typology for most essays on nationalism. Essays on the diverse forms of nationalism should not merely describe the differences, but should explain why they often strongly oppose each other.

✔ Essay questions on nationalism often ask about its paradoxes: forward- and backward-looking, a force for peace and a force for conflict, appealing to freedom and also endangering it, etc.

✔ Short questions often ask about similarities and differences between 'nation' and 'race', but racialism itself is rarely the subject of essay questions.

Feminism is a philosophy which advocates — at least — equality of rights between the sexes, otherwise known as **gender equality**. Originally an eighteenth- and nineteenth-century movement of middle-class women seeking the vote, it has developed into a wider and more far-reaching women's movement with diverse sub-strands including liberal feminism, socialist feminism and radical feminism.

> **Gender equality** — social and cultural equality of status between men and women, which most feminists seek.

'First wave' feminism

- When seventeenth- and eighteenth-century philosophers such as John Locke and Thomas Paine asserted 'the rights of *man*', they meant exactly that; as did the American Declaration of Independence (1776) that 'We hold these truths to be self-evident; that all *men* are created equal...'.

- Hence the emergence of so-called 'first wave' feminism, with Mary Wollstonecraft's *Vindication of the Rights of Women* (1792) and J.S. Mill and Harriet Taylor's 'Subjection of Women' (1869) which sought to reduce sexual discrimination primarily through a campaign for equal suffrage.

- This was a liberal variety of feminism.

- Wollstonecraft (incidentally, wife of the anarchist William Godwin and mother of Mary Shelley, the creator of Frankenstein) argued that women were, like men, essentially rational beings and therefore as capable of self-determination and as deserving of liberty, rights and, above all, education.

Achievements of 'first wave' liberal feminism — Revised

Mill's essay encouraged the government of the day to pass the Married Women's Property Act 1870 which, for the first time, gave married women the right to own property; previously, everything they possessed legally belonged to their husbands. By 1928, women had won the vote on equal terms with men in the UK.

Now test yourself — Tested

1 Define feminism, in a sentence.
2 Describe the origins of liberal feminism.
3 Name two 'first wave' liberal feminists.
4 List two achievements of 'first wave' liberal feminism.

Answers on p. 78

> **Examiner's tip**
> When exam questions ask you to explain the link between liberalism and feminism, it is not enough simply to say that there is such a thing as 'liberal feminism'; you should outline and explain the core liberal doctrines which lend themselves to a belief in equal rights for women — namely, individualism, rationalism, foundational and formal equality.

'Second wave' feminism

Liberal feminism Revised

- By the 1960s it was widely perceived that little had been done to reduce ongoing economic, political, legal and social inequalities between men and women: hence the emergence of 'second wave' feminism.
- Liberal feminists in the post-war era — such as Betty Friedan, whose book *The Feminist Mystique* (1963) marked the resurgence of feminist thinking in the 1960s — sought equal political and legal rights for women.
- Again, the core liberal values of individualism, rationalism and foundational and formal equality logically underpinned a reformist, progressive philosophy of liberal feminism.

Achievements of 'second wave' liberal feminism Revised

It made considerable strides in the UK, with legislation such as the Abortion Act 1967, Equal Pay Act 1970, Sex Discrimination Act 1976, the liberalisation of divorce, taxation and property laws, and the state provision of free and legal contraception. Women's whole lifestyles changed and even their health improved significantly as they bore fewer children, more safely. At around the same time in the US, liberal feminism went further and resulted in the legalisation of positive discrimination — i.e. quotas — for women as well as for ethnic minorities in education and employment.

However, the liberal feminist movement was predominantly white, Western and middle class and broadly excluded working-class and black women who were much more socially disadvantaged. Moreover, manifest gender inequalities across all classes persisted, and so more radical and even revolutionary forms of feminism emerged.

> **Now test yourself**
>
> 5 Why did 'second wave' feminism emerge?
>
> 6 Name one 'second wave' liberal feminist.
>
> 7 List three achievements of 'second wave' liberal feminism.
>
> Answers on p. 78
>
> Tested

Socialist feminism Revised

- Socialist feminism is largely based upon Marxist economic theory.
- The significance of economic factors in the sexual aspect of oppression was primarily asserted by Marx's collaborator Friedrich Engels in his book *The Origins of the Family, Private Property and the State* (1884).
- Socialist feminists have emphatically rejected the liberal feminist, reformist, approach, maintaining instead that sexual divisions in capitalism are due primarily to the operation of the economy, and therefore that a class revolution is the prerequisite of sexual equality.
- They argue that the orthodox nuclear family is an economic unit bound up with the male ownership and inheritance of private property. Women themselves have long been the property of men within the legal framework of marriage which, in turn, has been a contract between the male breadwinner and the housewife of

> **Typical mistake**
>
> It is wrong to assert that socialist feminism is purely Marxist; some utopian socialists, such as Charles Fourier, also advanced theories of female equality.

economic maintenance in return for sexual services. This is why, until the 1990s, there was no legal concept of rape within marriage.

- The traditional nuclear family — male breadwinner, female housewife — provides capitalism with 'two for the price of one', also providing men with an incentive to remain in exploitative work to support their families.

- Socialist feminists also stress the role of women as a 'reserve army of labour' in the event of an expansion of production such as in war. Women still provide a predominantly temporary and disposable source of labour, socially conditioned to accept low pay and status, thereby depressing wage levels without threatening men's jobs.

- Women's domestic work is also essential to the health and efficiency of the economy in sustaining and servicing their male partners, nurturing and conditioning future male workers and releasing men for employment.

- Marxist feminists emphasise the role of ideology and socialisation in perpetuating gender inequalities and women's acceptance of them.

- Therefore, for Marxists, women's liberation will be a by-product of economic and social revolution, and women should devote their time and energy to the class struggle rather than to bourgeois women's organisations.

> **Typical mistake**
>
> Do not focus exclusively on the socialist feminist analysis of the role of women in capitalism. They also argue that the traditional nuclear family structure facilitates the economic exploitation of male workers.

Radical feminism   Revised ☐

- Radical feminists, who emerged only in the second half of the twentieth century, go further than liberals and socialists to argue the primacy of gender divisions over all other social cleavages, including class and race.

- Writers such as Kate Millett and Shulamith Firestone argue that **patriarchy** — where the male is head of the household — in the personal and private sphere of home and family, has always been the first and most important power relationship in the human social system. They have effectively redefined 'politics' to apply it to this power relationship in the private sphere — hence their famous slogan, 'The personal is the political'.

- Patriarchy in the private sphere confines most women to the home and therefore largely excludes them from the public sphere of work, economics and politics, and is therefore the root of sexual inequality throughout society and, indeed, human history.

- Social conditioning in the private sphere of home and family inculcates gender roles into future generations. Hence radical feminists draw a basic distinction between '**sex**' — biological differences deriving from nature — and '**gender**' — socially constructed roles which both men and women internalise through conditioning from birth, but which can be changed: 'Biology is not destiny'.

> **Patriarchy** — literally, rule by the father; more generally, male dominance and female subordination throughout society.

> **Typical mistake**
>
> Students sometimes confuse the terms 'patriarchy' and 'patriotism'!

> **Typical mistake**
>
> When students are asked to explain the radical feminist slogan 'The personal is the political', they often wrongly assert that radical feminists are trying to bring politics, in the conventional sense, into the private sphere — e.g. political campaigns to improve the role of women in the home. This indicates a misunderstanding of the radical feminist use of the word 'politics'.

> **Sex** — innate biological differences between men and women.
>
> **Gender** — socially constructed and conditioned roles which are changeable.

> **Examiner's tip**
>
> When exam questions ask why radical feminists proclaim that 'the personal is the political', it is important to state explicitly that they have redefined 'politics' away from its conventional meaning of state and government in the public sphere.

- Hence radical feminists reject the '**public-private split**' — the divide between 'public man' and 'private woman'. For them, the priority is consciousness-raising amongst women towards a sexual revolution which will transform gender roles and eliminate private patriarchy.

The concept of patriarchy
Revised

How and why have feminists used the concept of patriarchy?

Due to their belief that conventional political theory has failed to see female oppression as a significant political fact, feminists have been forced to develop theories which see female oppression as a crucial, often primary, feature of human society.

However, different feminists use the concept of patriarchy differently:

- Liberal feminists associate patriarchy with legal and political oppression and the unequal distribution of rights in the public sphere. They believe that women should gain equal access to the public realm and therefore campaign for more women in senior economic and political positions.

- Socialist feminists attribute patriarchy to the capitalist economy and seek an economic revolution towards common ownership.

- The value of the concept of patriarchy from a radical feminist perspective is that it highlights the systematic, institutionalised and pervasive nature of male domination, suggesting, in the process, that this stems from and reflects the dominance of the husband-father within the family. Challenging gender inequality therefore requires a sexual revolution or qualitative social change through the overthrow of patriarchy in the private realm as well as in the public realm.

Feminist views on the 'public-private split'
Revised

- Liberal feminists: do not want to eradicate the public-private split because they believe in maintaining women's personal freedom of choice about their domestic role and they fear that encroaching on the private sphere could mean creeping totalitarianism.

- Socialist feminists: believe that patriarchy originates in the public sphere and thus spreads to the private sphere.

- Radical feminists: believe that patriarchy originates in the private sphere and thus spreads to the public sphere.

8   List three sub-strands of feminism and give one name associated with each.
9   Give three ways in which, according to socialist feminism, the capitalist economy benefits from the traditional nuclear family structure.
10 What do radical feminists mean by 'patriarchy'?
11 Explain the radical feminist slogan, 'The personal is the political'.
12 Why do most feminists differentiate between sex and gender?

Answers on p. 79

Difference feminism   Revised

- Most feminists subscribe to '**androgyny**' — the belief that biological sex is irrelevant to people's social and cultural roles — and pursue varying types and degrees of equality between men and women.

- A small sub-strand of radical feminism, however, argues that there are essential differences between men and women — that biology is destiny and it does and should shape social and cultural roles. This '**essentialist**' perspective argues that innate genetic and hormonal differences make men naturally more competitive and aggressive and women naturally more caring, nurturing and empathetic.

- Women therefore cannot and should not seek equality with men. They should not be 'male identified'. They should celebrate the distinctive traits of the female sex and seek liberation as fulfilled women.

- Some of these essentialists choose to practise lesbian separatism as a political strategy.

- The implication — often unstated — is that women's nature is not only different but superior to men's.

- Other feminists, including most radical feminists, therefore reject difference feminism as simply an inverted form of sexism.

Androgyny — the belief that humans are 'sexless' in the sense that biological factors are irrelevant to their social status.

Essentialism — the belief that biological factors are crucial in determining social, cultural and psychological traits.

Typical mistake

It is too sweeping and simplistic to assert that all 'difference feminists' seek female supremacy and matriarchy.

Examiner's tip

When exam questions ask about diverse schools of ecologism (see Chapter 7), point out that 'eco-feminism' is linked to essentialism and argues that women's natural traits of caring and nurturing make them better stewards of the environment and planet than are men.

Contrasts and conflicts within feminist thought

The public-private split   Revised

Radical feminists reject the 'public-private split' — the idea that there is, or should be, a division between the spheres of public, economic and political activity and the private arena of home and family — a split which liberals accept and even value. Whereas liberal feminists believe that encroaching upon the private sphere may amount to creeping totalitarianism, for radical feminists the priority is a sexual revolution in the private sphere which will eliminate private patriarchy.

Marxist feminists are closer to radicals than to liberals on this point: i.e. they reject the public-private split; but they argue that inequality is rooted in the public, rather than the private, sphere, and change must therefore begin in the wider economic system. For Marxists, gender explanations of women's inequality cut across class; socialist groups therefore face the particular, practical problem of whether women should maintain their own separate organisations distinct from the main (and mainly male) proletarian party. Modern Marxist feminists have increasingly recognised the complex interplay of economic, social and cultural factors in determining patterned, social inequalities, including those of both class and gender. This perception was the basis of Juliet Mitchell's revisionist work, *Women's Estate* (1971). She argued that social revolution was a necessary, but not sufficient, prerequisite of sexual equality and that the role of women as child-bearers, child-rearers and as sex objects would also have to be addressed.

> **Typical mistake**
>
> When students are asked about contrasts and conflicts across feminism, they often neglect to address potential conflicts *within* particular schools of feminism, such as tensions within socialist feminism.

Reformist or revolutionary?

Revised

Whereas liberals are inherently reformist, Marxist and radical feminists are both revolutionary — but they disagree on whether class or sexual revolution is the priority. They all agree that biological, economic and cultural factors all play a role in gender inequality but they disagree on the relative importance of those factors, and upon the solutions. For example, even liberals have long recognised that socialisation is a key factor in constructing gender roles: as J.S. Mill put it well over a century ago, 'I deny that anyone knows, or can know, the nature of the two sexes.... What is now called the nature of women is an eminently artificial thing — the result of forced repression' (1859). Nevertheless, liberals do not seek to challenge private family and marriage roles and relationships, whereas radicals see these as the root cause of sexual inequality.

Radical feminists, however, differ amongst themselves over whether women should — in a clear play on Marxist terminology — 'seize control of the means of reproduction' (Firestone) e.g. test-tube babies; or should pursue political separatism, e.g. women-only consciousness-raising groups and activities; or — at the most radical — should pursue private as well as public separatism in the form of political lesbianism. As the graffiti has put it for over 30 years, 'A woman needs a man like a fish needs a bicycle'. Radical feminism has also spawned anarcho-feminists and eco-feminists with their own particular concerns about the state and the environment. A few of the radicals insist upon the superiority of female traits and values — so-called 'supremacists' whose goal is matriarchy rather than equality. The most radical of the radicals have provided the focus or target for the crude political and tabloid stereotypes of hairy man-haters in dungarees, which have helped to ridicule and marginalise the very word 'feminism' since the 1980s.

Cultural diversity

Black and third-world feminists, meanwhile, stress the great diversity of women in and across cultures, and often criticise first-world feminists of all schools for racism. The experiences of a successful, white, Western, professional woman would be utterly alien to a black, working-class woman battling against racism and poverty as well as sexism.

Now test yourself

Tested

13 List three differences between liberal feminism and Marxist feminism.

14 List three differences between liberal feminism and radical feminism.

15 List three differences between Marxist feminism and radical feminism.

Answers on p. 79

Examiner's tip

When exam questions ask about differences between the diverse schools of feminism, you should make the differences explicit — 'X believes A whereas Y believes B' — and you should explain in what ways X criticises Y and vice versa.

Anti-feminism and 'post-feminism'

Anti-feminism

Revised

There will, of course, always be anti-feminists, such as traditional conservatives and fascists who believe that gender hierarchy is natural, functional, inevitable and desirable. Conservatism can even produce inverted chauvinism, e.g. the glorification of the wife/mother stereotype. The irony is that some self-proclaimed contemporary 'feminists' come very close to this stance: Germaine Greer and Betty Friedan, for example, in their later writings have rejected the goal of androgyny where men's and women's roles would not be socially differentiated, and have celebrated the unique nature of womanhood and the superior roles of motherhood and domesticity — much to the disgust of many other feminists.

'Post-feminism'

Revised

Some commentators — usually conservative journalists, whether male or female — have argued that feminism has done its job so effectively that it is now obsolete. 'Feminism is no longer necessary because it has become a victim of its own success' (Anne Applebaum, *New Statesman*, January 1998). She argues that inequality before the law no longer exists (though she admits that reality does not always match the letter of the law); and she argues that further changes — in attitudes and prejudices, for example — cannot be achieved by legislation or activism but only by time. Katie Roiphe (*Sunday Times*, March 1998) similarly says that feminism has succeeded to the extent that women now have to search desperately for 'trivial definitions of victimhood' like being complimented on their appearance or having doors opened for them by men.

Revision activity

Write a list of the quotations and slogans contained in this chapter, say to which school of feminism each one belongs, and decide how you would use each one in exam answers.

Now test yourself

Tested

16 Why do traditional conservatives believe that gender hierarchy is natural?

17 What is meant by 'post-feminism'?

18 List three problems or criticisms of feminism.

Answers on p. 79

Examiner's tip

When exam questions ask whether there can be such a thing as conservative feminism, stress in your answer that it is the organic doctrine of traditional and neo-conservatism which is fundamentally incompatible with feminism. Remember, however, that neo-liberalism logically embraces liberal feminism.

Revision activity

Devise a plan — either a written bullet-point summary or a mind map — for the following 45-minute essay title: 'Feminism is defined by the belief that "the personal is the political".' Discuss.

Typical mistake

When students are explaining why traditional and neo-conservatives are anti-feminist, they often address only the belief in 'tradition', but this is too simplistic.

Exam practice

A Short-answer questions

1 Explain the link between feminism and liberalism.

2 Why is the distinction between sex and gender so important to feminist analysis?

3 Why have radical feminists proclaimed that 'the personal is the political'?

B Essay questions

4 Analyse similarities and differences between liberal feminism and radical feminism.

5 'There are liberal feminists, socialist feminists and radical feminists, but no conservative feminists.' Discuss.

6 To what extent is feminism a single doctrine?

Answers and quick quiz 6 online

Online

Examiner's summary

✔ Short questions often focus on one school of feminist thought; essay questions usually require comparisons and contrasts of the three main schools of feminism — liberal, socialist and radical.

✔ Liberal and socialist feminism can be explained by reference to the core doctrines of liberalism and socialism themselves, such as rationalism and collectivism respectively.

✔ Each school of feminism emerged out of perceived deficiencies with previous schools, so it is often helpful to place them chronologically in essays.

✔ Essays on the diverse schools of feminist thought should not merely describe the differences, but should explain why they often strongly oppose each other, by reference to their core doctrines on the causes and remedies of female inequality.

✔ All three schools of feminism recognise the concept of patriarchy, the role of socialisation and the difference between 'sex' and 'gender', but they may place different emphasis on their importance.

Ecologism, or environmentalism, are labels adopted by political movements which regard the protection of the environment as a primary goal.

There is dispute over the labels 'ecologism' and 'environmentalism' — see below.

Narrowly, **ecologism** is the belief that the environment should be protected in the interests of the human species — 'shallow ecology'. Broadly, it is the belief that all parts and aspects of nature — human, non-human and inanimate — are of equal value and are deserving of equal protection in their own right — 'deep ecology'.

There are several other sub-strands within ecologism, but one unifying theme is '**holism**' — the belief that the natural world can only be understood as an interrelated whole.

> **Holism** — the belief that the natural world can only be understood as a whole, by studying the complex and interdependent relationships among its parts.

The origins of ecologism

Origins ———————————————————————— Revised ☐

The word '**ecology**' was coined by a German zoologist and philosopher, Ernst Haeckel, in 1879. He applied the term *oekologie* to 'the relation of the animal both to its organic as well as its inorganic environment'. The word comes from the Greek *oikos*, meaning household, home or place to live. Thus ecology deals with the organism and its environment, including other organisms and general physical surroundings. Concerns about the environment first emerged in the Victorian era as social critics perceived the destructive impact of the industrial revolution, population growth and urbanisation.

> **Ecology** — (the study of) the relationships between living organisms and their environment.

Environmentalism began to develop as a significant trend within Western politics in the 1960s. A seminal text was Rachel Carson's *The Silent Spring* (1962), which exposed the dark side of science. It showed that DDT and other chemical pesticides were poisoning the environment.

> **Environmentalism** — a reformist and anthropocentric green perspective — shallow ecology.

Environmentalists often argue that quality of life is more important than economic growth. Their cause has been given impetus since the 1960s by: deforestation, land clearance and species loss, over-fishing, population growth, fuel depletion, nuclear leakages such as Chernobyl (1986), toxic wastes, acid rain, the greenhouse effect, depletion of the ozone layer, global warming, globalisation, and growing concerns over food safety, genetically modified foods and pollution.

Examiner's tip

In exam answers, always explain explicitly that you are using the term 'environmentalism' to refer specifically to shallow ecology.

Now test yourself

1 Distinguish between 'ecologism' and 'environmentalism'.
2 Who coined the word 'ecology'?
3 Who wrote *The Silent Spring*?
4 Define 'holism'.
5 List five environmental concerns.

Answers on p. 79

Tested

Shallow and deep ecology

Ecologism is the only political ideology which, in its paradigm form, challenges the assumption of all others about the primacy of human interests. However, there are widely varying degrees of radicalism within ecologism.

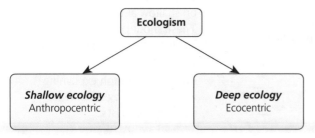

Figure 7.1 Shallow and deep ecology

Shallow ecology

Revised

The term '**shallow ecology**' was coined by Norwegian philosopher Arne Naess who founded deep ecology in 1972 and who also used the word 'environmentalism' disparagingly to refer to shallow ecologists — those whose concern with the natural environment is purely utilitarian and human-centred. They believe that the earth was given to human beings for their comfort and support and that the bounty of nature is the integral right of humanity. As John Locke said, 'We are the masters and possessors of nature'. They seek to preserve the environment because it nourishes our soil, cleanses our water and creates the very air which we breathe; and because, in the future, it may provide new foods, crops, fibres, antibiotics and other valuable products for human use.

Shallow ecologists are thus '**anthropocentric**' whereas deep ecologists are '**ecocentric**'. Anthropocentric views put human interests at the centre of their concerns for the environment, whereas ecocentric or biocentric views centre on the well-being of nature or the planet as a whole.

> **Deep/shallow ecologism** — ecocentric versus anthropocentric green ideologies.

> **Anthropocentrism** — the belief that human interests are of primary importance; the opposite of ecocentrism.
>
> **Ecocentrism** — the belief that the ecological interests of the planet are of primary importance; the opposite of anthropocentrism.

Examiner's tip

If a short exam question asks about the difference between anthropocentrism and ecocentrism, point out in your answer that all political philosophies, with the sole exception of deep ecology, are anthropocentric.

Deep ecology

Deep ecologists adopt the biocentric or ecocentric view that all living things are of equal value and worthy of moral respect in their own right and for their own sakes, and that the human species is no more important than any other. Indeed, insofar as most of the blame for the present environmental crises can be laid at the door of mankind, humans are the most damaging, destructive and dangerous species on the planet.

Deep ecologists condemn environmentalism as no more than a form of engineering which treats the environment as a resource to be manipulated and consumed whilst seeking to minimise pollution and other adverse effects upon humans.

Deep ecologists reject all conventional political philosophies as anthropocentric and human-centred, obsessed with mass production and limitless economic growth.

> **Typical mistake**
>
> It is wrong to assert that deep ecologists seek radical social change because, for them, this does not go far enough — they seek a paradigm shift in humanity's relationship with the environment.

> **Typical mistake**
>
> It is easy to be dismissive of deep ecology's belief in the moral parity of all living creatures, but do not be derisive or flippant about it in exam answers.

> **Examiner's tip**
>
> It is safe to assert in exam answers that, for deep ecologists only, ecologism begins where anthropocentrism ends.

> **Revision activities**
>
> - Create two cue cards: one each on shallow and deep ecology. These should describe the key features of each school of thought.
> - Write a paragraph explaining why deep ecologists criticise shallow ecologists.

Now test yourself

6 Define 'anthropocentrism'.

7 Define 'ecocentrism'.

8 Give another word for 'ecocentric'.

9 Who coined the terms 'shallow' and 'deep' ecology?

10 Who said, 'We are the masters and possessors of nature', and which school of ecologism does this express?

Answers on p. 79

Anti-industrialism

Industrialism

'**Industrialism**' describes economic and social systems based upon the mass, mechanised manufacture of goods rather than upon agriculture, craftsmanship or commerce. Environmentalist critics of industrialism argue that its noxious effluents have had a damaging impact upon the ecosystem.

> **Industrialism** — an economy based upon mass manufacturing rather than agriculture, handicrafts or commerce.

> **Typical mistake**
>
> It is an overstatement to say that all ecologists criticise industrialism; eco-capitalists (see later) believe that industrial technology and the free market can provide solutions to environmental problems.

Shades of green

The terms 'light green' and 'dark green' are frequently employed within the ecology movement but — like the terms 'environmentalism' and 'ecology' — they are used in different ways by different sources. Many simply equate 'light green' with 'shallow ecology' or 'environmentalism'; and 'dark green' with 'deep ecology'.

Others, however, use the terms 'light green' and 'dark green' to refer to strategic and tactical differences *within* the environmentalist or shallow ecology movement. Whereas the distinction between shallow and deep ecology centres on ends, the difference between light and dark greens centres on means.

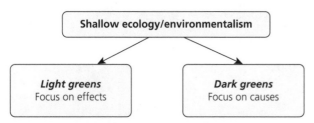

Figure 7.2 Light and dark greens

Light greens
Revised

By this usage, light greens deal with the effects, but not the causes, of ecological crises. They respond to specific environmental problems but do not question conventional assumptions about the inherent merits of industrialisation and economic growth. They believe in the economics of **sustainability**, whereby economic development can be compatible with environmental protection.

Sustainability — the process whereby economic development is able to progress over time without depleting resources and the natural environment.

Current examples of light green initiatives in the UK

- Investment in low-carbon technologies — praised by Western politicians for stimulating economic growth.
- Environmental taxes e.g. on air flights, 'gas-guzzling' cars and oil companies.
- Local waste recycling schemes.
- Water metering, rainfall harvesting and greywater recycling.
- Political pressures on wasteful water firms.
- Media campaigns on energy-saving measures for consumers.

Examiner's tip

Exam questions sometimes ask why and how ecologists have supported the principle of sustainability. For a full answer, you should specify which ecologists favour sustainability, and remember to address both the 'why' and the 'how' parts of the question.

Dark greens
Revised

Dark greens are committed environmentalists. They take seriously propositions about the finitude of the planet. They have a comprehensive political and moral critique of modern industrial societies, and a set of prescriptions concerning what a sustainable society would look like. Although they are still anthropocentric, putting human interests first, they go further in challenging or, indeed, rejecting, the intrinsic virtue of economic growth and contemporary concepts of economic and social 'progress'.

Difference between light and dark greens

Revised

One example often cited to illustrate the difference between these two perspectives is the campaign for lead-free petrol, which eventually persuaded the UK government to introduce a tax-incentive system — a major success from a light-green perspective. For dark greens, however, this did not begin to tackle the major issues of resource depletion and pollution — indeed, it might actually have been counterproductive in encouraging more car use and fuel consumption.

Now test yourself

Tested

11 Why do ecologists object to industrialism?
12 Define 'light green' environmentalism and give one example.
13 Define 'dark green' environmentalism and give one example.

Answers on p. 79

Ecology and ethics

Hard and soft ecology

Revised

Yet another distinction within ecologism is between '**hard**' and '**soft**' **ecology** (concepts coined by writer on environmental ethics, Kristin Shrader-Frechette, in the 1990s). Hard ecology views itself as quantitative, objective and predictive — in other words, as a science; whereas soft ecology is qualitative, ethical and untestable — and sometimes embodied in religious faiths such as Buddhism. In science, the word 'soft' is usually used negatively to mean assertions and assumptions that are not verifiable. Soft ecology employs vague and value-laden concepts such as equilibrium and integrity; but such ecologists defend their principled moral stand and reject the cold amoralism of hard ecology.

> Hard/soft ecologism — scientific versus ethical green ideologies.

Ecological ethics

Revised

Ecological ethics include the following features:

- A critique of conventional ethical, and especially anthropocentric, thinking.
- Emphasis on biocentric equality and the intrinsic value of nature.
- Belief in animal rights and welfare.
- Care for the well-being of future generations.
- Post-materialism and post-industrialism.
- Freedom as self-actualisation.

Revision activity

Devise a diagram to illustrate the connections between the following schools of thought:
- shallow and deep ecology
- light and dark greens
- soft and hard greens

Now test yourself

Tested

14 Distinguish between 'hard' and 'soft' ecology.
15 List three distinctive ethical issues raised by ecologism.

Answers on p. 79

Typical mistake

It is wrong to assert that ecologism is the only political philosophy which believes in animal welfare and the interests of future generations.

Greens, left and right

- Ecologism — like nationalism or feminism — is one of those flexible ideas which can attach itself to, or emerge out of, many wider ideologies. There is an immense diversity of sub-strands of ecological thought, not only linking to the mainstream ideologies of liberalism, conservatism and socialism but ranging from eco-anarchism through eco-feminism to eco-fascism.
- Greens may, therefore, be reactionary, reformist, radical or revolutionary. Anyone can be green.
- Greens, therefore, usually like to reject the left/right model of political thought altogether, with slogans like 'Neither left nor right, but forwards'. They claim to be a distinctive ecological movement which rejects both capitalism and socialism because of the shared dedication of those economic systems to industrial growth.
- All the main UK parties now pay more than lip-service to green policy issues. However, all these are 'light green' — tough on carbon but not on the causes of carbon, to paraphrase — and hence, according to Greenpeace and the Green Party, all three main parties are 'irresponsible' in ignoring the big environmental issues.

Right-wing ecologisms Revised

Ecologism in the early twentieth century was largely a right-wing phenomenon, linked to nationalism, conservatism and even fascism. Right-wing ideologies often advocate ruralism, nature conservation, the organic virtues of land, soil, place and the romantic and often reactionary idylls of pastoralism, which may lend themselves to environmentalist beliefs.

Traditional conservatism

Traditional conservatism, with its emphasis on organicism and the preservation of traditional ways of life, leans easily to rural conservation. After 2005 especially, the UK Conservative Party put strong rhetorical emphasis upon a 'green-blue agenda': 'Vote blue, go green'. It is unsurprising that the UK Conservative Party has its strongest bases of popular support in the English countryside.

Nazism

In the inter-war period, German Nazism — with its 'blood and soil' doctrines — looked to nature as a source of biological and moral purity as well as healthy pleasure, and pursued a policy of 'ruralisation'. Famously, Hitler was a vegetarian, and experiments in organic farming were carried out at Dachau concentration camp. The Nazis were the first in Europe to set up nature reserves and reforested woodlands, and they explored alternative energy sources such as wind technology.

Eco-capitalism

In the 1980s, forms of 'eco-capitalism' developed out of New Right neo-liberalism, which argued in favour of free-market solutions such as pricing goods and services to reflect their environmental costs. However, green solutions often seem to require either human altruism or authoritarian government, both of which pose problems for neo-liberals.

In the post-war era, radical and revolutionary left-wing forms of environmentalism emerged, notably eco-socialism and eco-anarchism, advocating radical decentralisation, small-scale egalitarian, pastoral and craft communes and grass-roots participatory (rather than representative) democracy. However, some forms of eco-socialism advocate a strong state to take on the massive power of the multinational corporations and to regulate the enforcement of environmentalist policies. Like right-wing ecologism, therefore, left-wing ecologism may be libertarian or authoritarian.

Eco-socialism

Eco-socialism explains environmental damage in terms of capitalism's rapacious thirst for profit. They extend the Marxist critique of capitalism as a system of mass exploitation by perceiving capitalism also as a system through which nature and other species are exploited. However, eco-socialism may be perceived as a contradiction in terms in that socialism, as a manifestation of the 'super-ideology' of industrialism, is guilty of the same materialist and pro-production priorities as is capitalism. 'Communist' regimes of the twentieth century, such as the USSR and China, have often done profound damage to the environment in the name of economic 'progress'. Eco-socialists also disagree on whether the environmental crisis or the class struggle should take priority. Finally, deep ecologists view socialism as anti-ecological because it is anthropocentric.

Eco-anarchism

Eco-anarchism has roots going back to nineteenth-century anarchists such as Peter Kropotkin, and anarchists such as Murray Bookchin were prominent in the emerging environmentalist movements of the 1960s. Eco-anarchism sees nature as providing a model of spontaneous and unregulated balance, harmony, growth and diversity which humans should emulate in the form of '**social ecology**'. Eco-anarchists are sometimes drawn to other holistic philosophies which emphasise oneness and natural interdependence, such as Gaia, Buddhism and Taoism. If, however, severe restrictions upon people's economic activities are needed to conserve the environment, it may require a strong state to enforce them — a problem for both eco-anarchists and liberals.

Eco-feminism

The radical feminist movement produced a strand of essentialist 'eco-feminism' (a term coined in the 1970s), which argued that women were essentially closer to nature than men (with stronger traits of caring, nurturing, emotion and empathy) and would be better stewards of the environment. Eco-feminists such as Mary Daly argue that environmental damage is the product of patriarchy (male dominance in society at large) and men's desire to be masters of nature. Women as child-bearers also have a stronger natural concern for the future of the environment. By this view, biology is destiny.

> **Social ecology** — the theory that human society operates according to ecological principles, implying a belief in natural harmony and the need for a balance between humans and nature.

> **Examiner's tip**
> If an exam question asks for an explanation of the link between ecologism and anarchism, the key concept is 'social ecology'.

> **Typical mistake**
> When writing about deep versus shallow ecology, students often neglect to mention the broad range of sub-strands within shallow ecology itself.

Diversity of view in ecologism

Revised

Environmentalism and ecologism are thus, perhaps, the most diverse and wide-ranging of all political ideologies, spanning left and right – and, sometimes, not clearly either left or right. This fact may, itself, pose some problems for ecologism.

Examiner's tip

Many exam essay questions on ecologism hinge upon how broadly the term itself is being employed.

Now test yourself

Tested

16 List (a) three right-wing schools of ecologism and (b) three left-wing schools of ecologism.

17 What is the main philosophical link between traditional conservatism and environmentalism?

18 What is the main philosophical link between neo-liberalism and environmentalism?

19 Why do deep ecologists view socialism as anti-ecological?

20 What is meant by 'social ecology'?

21 Name one eco-feminist.

Answers on pp. 79–80

Revision activity

Compile a table giving a brief description of each of the schools of shallow ecology listed below:
- Light green
- Dark green
- Traditional conservatism
- Eco-capitalism
- Eco-socialism
- Eco-anarchism

Exam practice

A Short-answer questions

1 Distinguish between anthropocentrism and ecocentrism.

2 How have ecologists revised conventional notions of morality?

3 On what grounds have some ecologists supported capitalism?

B Essay questions

4 Is ecologism entirely incompatible with modern industrial society?

5 'Ecologists fundamentally reject all conventional political creeds.' Discuss.

6 To what extent is ecologism a single doctrine?

Answers and quick quiz 7 online

Online

Examiner's summary

✔ 'Ecologism' and 'environmentalism' are labels adopted by political movements which regard the protection of the environment as an important goal. There is dispute over the usage of the labels 'ecologism' and 'environmentalism'. Students should use 'ecologism' in its broadest sense, and 'environmentalism' to mean shallow ecology.

✔ Contemporary ecologism emerged in the 1960s with growing awareness of environmental problems.

✔ The main split within the philosophy is between shallow ecology — anthropocentrism; and deep ecology — ecocentrism.

✔ Deep ecology is a paradigm shift in political philosophy, as it is the only school of thought to reject the primacy of human interests.

✔ There are multiple sub-strands of shallow ecology, spanning left and right schools of political thought, scientism and spiritualism, libertarianism and authoritarianism.

The exam specification describes **multiculturalism** as 'an 'area' of ideological disagreement rather than, necessarily, a coherent ideology in its own right'. These notes aim to outline and explain the different usages of the term and the different political attitudes — positive and negative — towards it.

> **Multiculturalism** — the policies or processes whereby the distinctive identities of the cultural groups within a society are maintained or supported.

Definition
Revised

According to the Oxford Dictionary, a 'culture' is 'the customs, civilization and achievements of a particular time or people'; and 'multicultural', therefore, literally just means 'many cultures'. As commentators often point out, the UK has always housed diverse cultures: centuries ago, for example, many people lived in the countryside and killed rabbits, while others lived in towns and went shopping; upper-class people had very different lifestyles and customs from working-class people, and so on. In this sense, multiculturalism in the UK is much older than democracy.

As a political viewpoint, however, 'multiculturalism' implies approval of cultural **diversity** within a society as a catalyst for self-worth, mutual tolerance, social vibrancy and broader social unity — 'diversity within unity' (Andrew Heywood, *Political Ideologies*, 2012). It also assumes reference to national, religious or racial differences rather than class, geographic or demographic distinctions. The term only became commonplace in political debate in the 1990s; although the term 'multiculturalism' was first used in Canada in 1965 to describe an accepting and encouraging approach to bilingualism within the country.

> **Diversity** — difference; variety; multiformity.

Multiculturalism can therefore mean:

- A descriptive term for racial, ethnic, cultural and linguistic diversities within a society.
- A normative term for the positive endorsement of cultural diversity, recognition of the rights of diverse groups and celebration of the benefits to society which such diversity brings. This is its political or 'ideological' usage.
- Government endorsements of cultural diversity: for example, the political accommodation of post-immigration minorities, either in public policy or institutional structures.

> **Examiner's tip**
>
> When answering essay questions beginning 'To what extent' — for example, 'To what extent can multiculturalism be reconciled with national unity and cohesion?' — the answer is always 'To some extent'.

> **Examiner's tip**
>
> Exam answers on this topic — especially essays — should bear in mind all three interpretations of 'multiculturalism' listed here.

Now test yourself
Tested

1 Distinguish between the descriptive and the normative usages of the term 'multiculturalism'.

2 Where and when was the normative use of 'multiculturalism' first employed?

Answers on p. 80

Origins and development of multiculturalism

Development ———————————————————————————————— Revised

- Multiculturalism first emerged as an ideological viewpoint in the 1960s' US black consciousness movement. It often took the form of 'ethnocultural nationalism' — a form of nationalism with a particularly proud sense of ethnic and cultural roots — and it sought to challenge economic, social and often racial disadvantage and discrimination. This political assertion of minority cultural identities was quite new.
- Cultural diversity in Western democracies was enhanced by post-war increases in migration which were, in turn, generated by: the need for new workers in a time of economic boom; then a wave of refugees due to wars and the break-up of states like the Soviet Union and Yugoslavia; and finally by economic **globalisation**.
- There was a growing recognition that multicultural societies had become an irreversible fact. By the early 2000s, therefore, most Western states had officially embraced multiculturalism as an ideology into public policy.
- Global terrorism and the rise of radical Islam within Western states have strengthened calls for multicultural politics to keep extremism at bay; but many opponents argue, conversely, that multiculturalism may simply allow, or even legitimise, such extremism.

> **Globalisation** — the increasing interdependence and integration of national economies, cultures and polities.

> **Typical mistake**
> 'Globalisation' is often employed purely in economic terms, but remember that it has political and cultural dimensions as well.

Now test yourself ———————————————————— Tested

3 Give three reasons for the growing cultural diversity in post-war Western democracies.

4 Explain the ambivalent relationship between 'multiculturalism' and 'extremism'.

Answers on p. 80

Features of multiculturalism

Post-colonialism ———————————————————————————————— Revised

After 1945, **post-colonialist** attitudes sought to challenge Eurocentrism and the cultural hegemony of Western imperial ideas and assumptions. It rejected the universalist pretensions of Western liberal ideology.

> **Post-colonialism** — assertions of cultural identity after the independence of former colonies.

Examples of post-colonialism include:

- Gandhi's Indian nationalism
- 1960s' black nationalism
- Edward Said's book *Orientalism* (1978)

Identity politics

Identity politics perceives people in terms of their cultural characteristics and stresses the importance of factors such as language, religion and ethnicity in shaping personal and social identity. It may go as far as 'particularism': the belief that cultural differences between people and societies are more important than what they have in common — a perspective which again challenges the universalist assumptions of liberalism. It seeks to promote the awareness and interests of those groups in the face of perceived social injustice. Culture is important in giving people a sense of rootedness, and diverse identities — whether of religion, language or racial ancestry — should be celebrated. Multiculturalism is, therefore, collectivist and **communitarian** and thus largely opposed to liberal individualism.

> **Identity politics** — the pursuit of group interests defined by collective identity and common experience (for example, of culture, race or gender).
>
> **Communitarianism** — the belief that people's identity and common values are shaped by the social groups to which they belong, rather than by atomistic individualism.

Minority rights

Minority rights are collective entitlements of representation, self-government and legal protections (e.g. of dress codes or religious holidays) — often including reverse or 'positive' discrimination in education, work or political representation (called 'affirmative action' in the USA). They have generated controversial questions of apology or compensation for past disadvantage or discrimination (e.g. slavery). These are group rights rather than individual rights. They are 'special' rights because they are specific to particular cultural groups and because they may grant advantages to those groups which are not enjoyed by the wider society.

> **Minority rights** — the individual and especially collective entitlements of marginalised groups in society.

They are controversial because:

- They may hinder integration of cultural groups into wider society (e.g. the issue of the veil for Muslim women).
- Positive discrimination is often perceived as unfair and counter-productive.
- The right not be offended has prompted, for example, the UK to introduce a law banning expressions of religious hatred, but this conflicts with liberal notions of freedom of expression.
- There are inevitable tensions between minority group rights and individual rights — including whether individuals have the right to opt in or out of a culture such as Islam.

Diversity

This is the belief that cultural differences are compatible with citizenship and social/political cohesion. Whereas nationalists largely believe that citizenship should be based on cultural homogeneity, multiculturalism believes that a denial of cultural diversity may generate resentment, isolation and extremism.

However:

- There is a risk that encouraging cultural diversity may weaken people's sense of their own cultural identity.

- There are fears that it may also undermine social stability or political unity. For both of these reasons, conservatives are generally hostile to multiculturalism because they believe that humans are psychologically insecure creatures who need a strong sense of common cultural identity, which is also a prerequisite for social order and stability.

Now test yourself Tested ☐

5 Define 'post-colonialism' and give two examples.
6 Define 'identity politics'.
7 Give two reasons why 'identity politics' contradicts liberal values.
8 Define 'minority rights'.
9 Give three reasons why minority rights are controversial.
10 Give two reasons why cultural diversity may be controversial.

Answers on p. 80

Types of multiculturalism

Liberal multiculturalism — Revised ☐

Liberal multiculturalism embodies a belief in individual freedom to cherish and celebrate one's distinctive cultural identity and, above all, in tolerance of cultural differences and disagreements. This reflects the liberal beliefs in human rationalism, freedom of choice in the moral sphere and the view that truth prevails in a free market of ideas.

However:

- Liberal tolerance is not morally neutral; it only extends to cultures which are, themselves, tolerant and rights-oriented; it may not extend, for example, to female circumcision or forced marriages. With no trace of irony, UK PM Tony Blair told Muslims in Britain after the London 2005 bombings that tolerance was a must: 'Conform to it,' he said, 'or don't come here'. He added, 'The right to be different. The duty to integrate. That is what being British means'.

- Liberal multiculturalism also requires a liberal democratic framework, and may not support calls for the creation of other political systems, such as an Islamic state based on sharia law.

- Liberal multiculturalism also regards cultural identity as largely a matter of private choice, but believes that integration and inclusion should be the norm in the public sphere — for example, proficiency in English and knowledge of British history in the UK, or the ban on religious dress and symbols in French schools. For some other multiculturalists, this is an attack on multiculturalism itself.

- The liberal emphasis on individual rights conflicts with multiculturalism's emphasis on group rights.

- Pluralist multiculturalists (see below) perceive liberal multiculturalism as a superficial 'celebration of costumes, customs and cooking'.

Now test yourself

11 List three values of liberal multiculturalism.
12 Give two possible criticisms of liberal multiculturalism.

Answers on p. 80

Tested ☐

Pluralist multiculturalism

Revised

Pluralist multiculturalism goes further than liberal multiculturalism in accepting the equal validity and legitimacy of liberal, non-liberal and illiberal ideas and values, though they may be incompatible or even incomparable — a moral **pluralism** which implies a 'post-liberal' stance where liberal ideas and values can no longer claim moral supremacy (John Gray, *Liberalism*, 1995). 'Life may be seen through many windows' (Isaiah Berlin, *Four Essays on Liberty*, 1969). It criticises liberalism as being tainted by colonialism and racism.

However:

- Pluralist multiculturalism may undermine civic cohesion and social unity, especially where it takes the 'particularist' form of defending or even prioritising the identities and interests of groups perceived as oppressed or corrupted by decadent, colonial and racist Western culture.
- For liberals especially, pluralist multiculturalism poses the dilemma of how far to tolerate intolerant or oppressive beliefs.
- Moral pluralism may be premised on moral indifference, which may be dangerous.

> **Pluralism** — diverse and competing political groups, cultural beliefs or moral values; or a commitment to such diversity.

> **Examiner's tip**
>
> When answering one-sided short questions such as 'On what grounds have liberals criticised multiculturalism?' do not digress onto the other side of the argument. Essays, however, will always require both or all sides of the argument.

Now test yourself

Tested

13 How does pluralist multiculturalism differ from liberal multiculturalism?

14 Why might pluralist multiculturalism be 'dangerous'?

Answers on p. 80

Cosmopolitan multiculturalism

Revised

Cosmopolitan multiculturalism values cultural diversity insofar as different cultures can learn and share from each other, as a transitional step on the way to international identity and harmony or a world state.

However:

- Cosmopolitanism and multiculturalism are essentially conflicting ideas, because cosmopolitanism believes in international or global identity transcending particular cultures.
- Multiculturalism is, in fact, often a reaction against globalisation and the subsequent merging or submerging of national identities.
- Cosmopolitan multiculturalism, in turn, perceives society as a 'melting pot' or fusion of different values, traditions and lifestyles — 'hybridity' — which may fundamentally blur and weaken distinctive cultural identities.

> **Cosmopolitanism** — the advocacy of peaceful cooperation among nations and, ultimately, world citizenship.

> **Examiner's tip**
>
> Most essay answers may usefully be structured around the three key types of multiculturalism explained here.

> **Revision activity**
>
> Create three cue cards: one each on liberal, pluralist and cosmopolitan multiculturalism. These should contain key doctrines, definitions, dilemmas and mutual criticisms.

Now test yourself

Tested

15 Why is 'cosmopolitan multiculturalism' essentially a contradiction in terms?

Answers on p. 80

Critical perspectives on multiculturalism

Conservatism
Revised

Conservatives believe that security-seeking individuals and a stable society require cultural homogeneity. Multiculturalism is therefore a threat to social cohesion and majority interests, and 'diversity within unity' is a myth. **Assimilation** (the absorption of minority groups into the host culture) and restrictions on immigration, or even repatriation, are favoured by conservatives.

> **Assimilation** — absorption of a minority immigrant group and its adoption of the cultural norms of the host group.

Typical mistake

Students often explain conservative hostility to multiculturalism purely in terms of tradition, but it is primarily explained by the conservative belief in the psychological imperfection of humans.

Socialism (or 'social reformism')
Revised

Socialists argue that it is not a lack of cultural recognition which encumbers some groups but their lack of economic power and social status. From this perspective, multiculturalism is a form of 'divide and rule' of oppressed and exploited classes. It may distract or detract from redistributive and welfare politics and narrow people's sense of wider social responsibility. Marxism would call it a form of 'false consciousness'.

Revision activity

Do an internet search and find comments on multiculturalism from the leaders of each main political party to ascertain their ideological positions on it.

Liberalism
Revised

Multiculturalism is collectivist and, therefore, conflicts with liberal individualism. Its emphasis on the value of diversity and particularism conflicts with liberal universalism — the belief that certain values and entitlements are applicable to all people everywhere, regardless of culture, race or creed. Certain forms of multiculturalism may also impinge on human rights and freedoms, or on **toleration**. However, liberalism can incorporate specifically liberal forms of multiculturalism (see above).

> **Toleration** — acceptance or even welcoming of diverse views and values.

Feminism
Revised

Feminists object specifically to patriarchal cultures which legitimise and perpetuate the oppression of women in their power structures, family arrangements, moral or dress codes. Hence they object to multicultural perspectives which defend such cultures.

Now test yourself
Tested

16 Why are conservatives generally hostile to multiculturalism?
17 Why do socialists criticise the emphasis on cultural identity?
18 Give two possible dilemmas for liberal multiculturalism.
19 Which forms of culture do feminists reject?

Answers on p. 80

Revision activity

Devise a plan — either a written bullet-point summary or a mind map — for the following 45-minute essay title: '"Multiculturalism breeds tension and social conflict." Discuss'.

Exam practice

A Short-answer questions

1   In what sense is multiculturalism a form of communitarianism?

2   Why have some multiculturalists criticised liberalism?

3   Why have conservatives had reservations about multiculturalism?

B Essay questions

4   To what extent do multiculturalists support diversity and the politics of difference?

5   To what extent is multiculturalism compatible with liberalism?

6   Can multiculturalism be reconciled with any form of nationalism?

Answers and quick quiz 8 online

Online

Examiner's summary

✔ 'Multiculturalism' has descriptive, normative and policy interpretations and only became a common term in political debate in the 1990s.

✔ Growing cultural diversity in post-war Western democracies prompted many governments to adopt and endorse multicultural policies by the early 2000s.

✔ Key features of multiculturalism include post-colonialism, identity politics, minority rights and diversity.

✔ The three main schools of multicultural thought are liberal, pluralist and cosmopolitan multiculturalism; as well as challenging each other, they all have internal tensions and dilemmas.

✔ All of the mainstream political philosophies criticise multiculturalism, to varying degrees — even liberalism.

Now test yourself answers

Chapter 1

1 Liberals view human nature as rational but in a self-interested way.

2 Individualism believes in the primacy of the rights and freedoms of every individual over those of any group, society or state.

3 Every individual is of primary importance, is unique in his or her character and attributes and yet is as important as every other individual. Liberals therefore believe in foundational equality: that every individual, despite having different skills and talents, is of equal moral worth and is deserving of the same fundamental human rights.

4 Liberals believe that rational individuals are capable and deserving of exercising freedom responsibly.

5 'Over himself, over his own body and mind, the individual is sovereign.' (J.S. Mill)

6 'Constitutionalism' is the advocacy or acting within the framework of a constitution — a set of rules which set limits to government power.

7 'Pluralism' means diverse and competing sources of power in society, especially many parties and pressure groups. Liberals advocate pluralism to fragment power and to enhance freedom of choice.

8 Modern liberals, like classical liberals, continue to value negative freedom — non-interference — in the private sphere of home, family and personal morality.

9 'I may not agree with what you say, but I shall defend to the death your right to say it.' (F.M. Voltaire)

10 Liberals face a dilemma about how far to tolerate intolerance.

11

Limit to power	External check	Internal check
Constitutionalism	✓	
Bicameralism		✓
Pluralism		✓
Rule of law	✓	
Separation of powers		✓
Federalism		✓

12 A *laissez-faire* economy is free-market, private-enterprise economy with minimal state intervention.

13 John Locke advocated a 'nightwatchman state'.

14 By 'the invisible hand' Adam Smith meant the economic market forces of supply and demand.

15 Classical liberals favour economic inequality as an incentive to, and a measure of, enterprising effort.

16 'Egoistical individualism' emphasises the self-interested and self-reliant side of human nature.

17 Modern liberalism kept many of the main doctrines of classical liberalism, notably:
- The mechanistic theory of the state.
- A view of human nature as rational and self-interested, therefore corruptible.
- Belief in individual freedom.
- Belief in private property as a natural right.

18 The main difference between classical and modern liberalism concerns the degree of state intervention in the economy.

19 Modern liberals believe that the state has a positive and interventionist role in enhancing positive freedom in the economy.

20 The state can enhance positive freedom in health, education and welfare.

21 Liberals advocate:
- foundational equality
- formal equality
- equality of opportunity

22 All liberals reject the socialist doctrine of equality of outcome, because it treats unlike individuals alike and is therefore unjust.

23

Liberal doctrine	Classical liberalism	Modern liberalism
Free-market economy	✓	
Egoistical individualism	✓	
Developmental individualism		✓
Welfare		✓
Positive freedom		✓
Negative freedom	✓	

24 'Liberal democracy' is a form of representative government based on free, fair and competitive elections, pluralism, constitutionalism, the rule of law, civil liberties and a (free- or mixed-) market economy.

25 'Liberal democracy' may be a contradiction in terms because liberalism is an individualist philosophy, whereas democracy is a collectivist philosophy.

26 Liberals are wary of democracy because:
- Democracy implies majoritarianism — 'tyranny of the majority'.
- Democracy may therefore undermine individual sovereignty and minority rights.
- Democracy may give a voice to the uneducated, the ignorant and the propertyless.
- Democracy may threaten property rights.

27 Liberals favour democracy because:
- Power should be based upon legitimate authority.
- Consent is necessary for such legitimacy.

- The people can be a constraining influence upon the power of government and state.
- Democracy may help to ensure political representation.

28 New Right neo-liberalism.

29 'New' Labour's 'third way' and, to a lesser extent, social democracy, have been most influenced by liberal ideas.

Chapter 2

1 Intellectual imperfection requires reliance upon pragmatism, tradition, history and experience rather than upon abstract theories and doctrinaire ideologies. Moral imperfection requires law and order, religion and private property (because we are more likely to respect the property of others if we own property ourselves). Psychological imperfection requires traditional values, cultural homogeneity and private property, all to provide a sense of identity, security and stability.

2 The organic theory views inequality as natural and desirable.

3 Traditional conservatives value cultural homogeneity and unity due to their organic theory and humans' psychological need for security, identity and rootedness.

4 The organic society must be rooted in its past to flourish; humans have a psychological need for historical identity and rootedness; and if something has stood the test of time it should be left alone.

5 Traditional conservatives view humans as psychologically, intellectually and morally imperfect.

6 New Right neo-liberals view humans as rational and self-interested.

7 'There is no such thing as society — only individuals and families.' (Margaret Thatcher)

8 Tories value a practical approach to concrete circumstances because they mistrust humans' intellectual capacity to theorise and therefore they mistrust abstract theory.

9 New Right neo-liberals trust human rationality and therefore trust abstract theory and doctrinaire principles.

10 'No U-turns — the lady's not for turning.' (Margaret Thatcher)

11 Whereas traditional conservatives are organic paternalists, neo-conservatives are organic authoritarians.

12 Free economy, strong state in all other spheres.

13 A free-market economy may require strong law and order etc. to curb and control the social instabilities which it creates.

14 'The trouble with a free-market economy is that it takes so many police to make it work.' (Neal Ascherson)

15 Both traditional conservatism and neo-conservatism are organic theories which mistrust human nature.

16 The neo-liberal emphasis on the free market and on unconstrained property rights is much stronger than that of the traditional conservatives.

17 There is a clear difference between the Tory view of an organic, static, class hierarchy and the neo-liberal view of an individualist, competitive ladder of meritocracy.

18 Organic conservatives value law and order because they mistrust human nature.

19 John Locke (1632–1704) said that private property was a natural right, along with life and liberty.

20 **(a)** Noel O'Sullivan. It describes the organic conservative pessimistic view of human nature.

(b) Edmund Burke. It describes traditional conservative belief in tradition itself.

(c) Benjamin Disraeli. It describes a pragmatic reason for traditional conservative paternalist welfarism.

(d) Margaret Thatcher. It describes neo-liberal atomistic individualism.

Chapter 3

1 'Fundamentalist socialism' seeks to abolish capitalism entirely, whereas 'revisionist socialism' merely seeks to reform and tame capitalism.

2 Socialists view human nature as rational and altruistic — that is, as having concern for the welfare of others. However, it is also 'plastic' — moulded by circumstances.

3 Socialists believe that cooperation is more natural for altruistic humans than is competition; it is also more efficient and it promotes social harmony.

4 Socialists favour equality for the following reasons:

- Socialists believe that economic inequalities in capitalism are the result of systemic injustices.
- Equality would enhance positive freedom by safeguarding people from poverty and allowing them to flourish and fulfil their potential.
- Without social equality, other forms of equality — e.g. foundational and formal equality — are not possible. Socialists argue that liberals are deluding themselves on this point.
- Social equality would enhance social harmony and community.

5 Sir Thomas More.

6 A 'utopia' is a perfect, imaginary society.

7 Utopian socialists had a highly optimistic view of human nature and they advanced a moral critique of capitalism as based on exploitation, avarice and injustice.

8 Robert Owen (1771-1858) was a British utopian socialist.

9 Marxism is primarily an economic theory.

10 The two main classes in capitalism are the bourgeoisie — ruling class — and the proletariat — working class.

11 Exploitation is inevitable because it is the only possible source of new value and profit, which is the defining feature of capitalism.

12 'Dictatorship of the proletariat' means the transitional phase of rule by the majority working class after the revolution — a necessary but temporary stage to prevent bourgeois counter-revolution.

13 The state is the political agent of the economic ruling class in every class stage; therefore, when classes have been abolished, the state will no longer be needed.

14 'Evolutionary socialism' means parliamentary socialism.

15 Revolutionary socialists believe that the state is an irredeemable agent of bourgeois class rule, whereas evolutionary socialists believe that the state can be reformed to serve the working class.

16 Sidney Webb believed that, when the majority working class got the vote, socialism via the parliamentary road was arithmetically inevitable.

17 Three sub-strands of parliamentary socialism are democratic socialism, social democracy and the third way.

18 Socialists adopted the parliamentary road because:
- The working class got the vote.
- They largely rejected the likely violence of revolution.
- Capitalist states were increasingly strong and able to prevent revolution.

19 'Eurocommunism' was the label applied to the Western European communist parties from the 1970s to the 1990s when they adopted the parliamentary, pluralist route to communism.

20 Clause 4 of the UK Labour Party's founding constitution advocated common ownership.

21 Socialists have promoted collectivism in the following ways:
- Some utopian socialists such as Fourier and Owen set up experimental communes.
- Revolutionary socialists promote it via mass working-class uprising, collective ownership of the means of production and the abolition or disappearance of the state in favour of forms of direct democracy.
- Evolutionary socialists promote it via state nationalisation, redistribution through progressive taxation, extensive welfarism and trade union organisation, rights and activities.

22 'Revisionism' means revising and watering down the original and fundamental goals of the philosophy.

23 Socialism moved to the right after the Second World War for several reasons:
- The Cold War, which generated profound ideological hostility in the West towards any form of radical socialism.
- The post-war economic boom which meant that capitalism appeared to be delivering the goods in terms of increasing living standards and welfare for the working class.
- These economies were also changing shape: traditional 'blue-collar' industries were declining and the 'white-collar' service sector was growing. The traditional working class was diminishing in number, and the middle classes were increasing in number.

24

Democratic socialism	Social democracy
Radical	Reformist
More 'left wing'	More 'right wing'
Mainly collective economy	Mainly private economy
Equality	Freedom and fairness
Extensive welfare state	Extended welfare state
Anti-private health/education	Pro-choice

25 Neo-revisionism occurred in the 1990s, for the following reasons:
- The continuing shrinkage of the working class and growth of the middle class.
- Repeated election defeats — for example, four successive general election defeats of the British Labour Party 1979–97.
- The almost irreversible impact of New Right conservative ideology and policies since the 1970s.

26 The 'third way' was a neo-revisionist blend of free-market capitalism and state socialism.

Chapter 4

1 'Anarchy' in Greek originally meant 'no rule'.

2 All anarchists broadly agree on: faith in human nature; the primacy of freedom; rejection of the state; the need for direct democracy.

3 'Perfectibility is the most unequivocal characteristic of the human species.' (William Godwin, 1793)

4 Anarchists reject orthodox forms of representative democracy, dismissing them as a sham and a facade where voters surrender their personal autonomy and thus collude in their own oppression.

5 Anarchists believe that the state is sovereign, compulsory, coercive, exploitative and destructive.

6 Anarchists believe that constitutionalism perpetuates the myth that the sovereign state can be limited and tamed.

7 Anarchists believe that consent is a myth, because we cannot opt in or out of state control.

8 Collectivist anarchists believe that humans are rational and altruistic, whereas individualist anarchists believe that humans are rational and self-interested.

9 The four sub-strands of anarchism are:
- Anarcho-communism.
- Anarcho-syndicalism.
- Egoism.
- Anarcho-capitalism.

10 Anarchists are 'utopian' in the positive sense that they are seeking a perfect future society; and in the negative sense that, according to critics, their goals are over-optimistic and unattainable.

11 Anarcho-communists envisage a radically decentralised society of small, egalitarian and self-governing communes which operate and interrelate on the basis of cooperation and communitarianism.

12 Peter Kropotkin, James Guillaume.

13 Max Stirner.

14 Murray Rothbard.

15 Anarchism and Marxism:
Similarities:
- Collectivist.
- Egalitarian.
- Revolutionary.

Differences:

- Marxism is 'scientific' whereas anarchism is 'utopian'.
- Marxism believes that the state is the superstructural agent of the ruling class, whereas anarchism believes that the state is the primary evil.
- Marxism believes that the state will wither away when classes are abolished, whereas anarchism believes that the state must be directly overthrown.

16 Anarchism and liberalism:

Similarities:

- Individualist.
- Liberating.
- Rationalist.

Differences:

- Liberals believe that the state is a necessary evil, whereas anarchists believe that the state is an unnecessary evil.
- Liberals believe in the 'rule of law', whereas anarchists believe that all law curtails liberty.
- Liberalism is reformist whereas anarchism is revolutionary.

17 Writing books, issuing pamphlets, demonstrations, acts of peaceful civil disobedience such as non-payment of taxes, riots, bombs.

Chapter 5

1 Nationalism is a sense of common cultural identity based upon factors such as language, religion, history, territory and ethnicity, often seeking to create or defend a sovereign state in which to house the nation.

2 ETA, IRA, Scottish Nationalist Party.

3 Nationalism originated in late eighteenth-century Europe, with the French Revolution and industrialisation.

4 National identity has at least three dimensions: cultural, political and psychological.

5 Whereas a state is a sovereign, political power over a given territory — which may be multi-national — a nation (a much more recent concept than the idea of the state) is a cultural entity, a collection of people with a shared sense of common heritage.

6 'Nation' and 'state' are often confused because:

(a) Some states are nation-states, i.e. sovereign territories housing a predominantly common culture.

(b) Most nations seek to achieve or maintain statehood.

7 The United Kingdom is a multicultural state.

8 Most nations seek statehood for one or more of three reasons:

(a) Self-determination, freedom and autonomy — especially true of liberal and anti-colonial nationalism.

(b) International peace and harmony — especially true of liberal nationalism.

(c) Domestic social stability and cohesion — especially true of conservative nationalism.

9 (a) Liberal nationalism: e.g. Scottish nationalism.

(b) Conservative nationalism: e.g. English nationalism.

(c) Chauvinist nationalism: e.g. Italian fascism.

(d) Anti-colonial nationalism: e.g. Palestinian nationalism.

10 (a) Patriotism: literally, love of the fatherland; a psychological attachment to one's nation or country.

(b) Xenophobia: an irrational fear or hatred of foreigners.

(c) Ethnocentrism: a sense, not only of cultural distinction, but also of inherent cultural superiority.

11 Anthony D. Smith described nationalism as a 'chameleon ideology' because it can adapt and attach itself to almost any wider philosophy.

12 Anarchism is most strongly anti-nationalist; socialism and liberalism are also wary of nationalism.

13 Political nationalism is defined by the principle of self-determination — e.g. Scottish nationalism — whereas cultural nationalism is associated with the defence of a nation's cultural heritage — e.g. Welsh nationalism.

14 Racialism is the belief that humans are divided into distinct biological and ethnic castes which can be ranked in a hierarchy and which have economic, political and/or social significance. Examples: South African apartheid, German Nazism, Ku Klux Klan.

15 Causes of racialism include economic insecurity, imperialism and lack of education.

16 Racialism highlights the liberal dilemma of how far to tolerate intolerance.

17 Anthony Smith's continuum illustrates a range of political ideologies between pure and mixed nationalism and racialism:

(a) Pure nationalism: e.g. SNP.

(b) Racial-nationalism (more nationalist than racialist): e.g. Italian fascism.

(c) National-racism (more racialist than nationalist): e.g. German Nazism.

(d) Pure racialism: e.g. Ku Klux Klan.

18 The British National Party may seek to blur the concepts of 'nation' and 'race'.

Chapter 6

1 Feminism is a philosophy which advocates — at least — equality of rights between the sexes.

2 Liberal feminism emerged in the eighteenth century in response to liberal thinkers' neglect of women's rights and freedoms.

3 Mary Wollstonecraft and John Stuart Mill.

4 'First wave' feminism of the liberal variety sought to reduce sexual discrimination primarily through a campaign for equal suffrage. It also won the Married Women's Property Act 1870.

5 By the 1960s it was widely perceived that little had been done to reduce ongoing economic, political, legal and social inequalities between men and women. Hence the emergence of 'second wave' feminism.

6 Betty Friedan.

7 The Abortion Act 1967, Equal Pay Act 1970, Sex Discrimination Act 1976, the liberalisation of divorce,

taxation and property laws, and the state provision of free and legal contraception.

8 Liberal feminism: Betty Friedan. Socialist feminism: Friedrich Engels. Radical feminism: Kate Millett.

9 Three ways in which, according to socialist feminism, the capitalist economy benefits from the traditional nuclear family structure:

- Socialist feminists argue that the orthodox nuclear family is an economic unit bound up with the male ownership and inheritance of private property.
- The traditional nuclear family — male breadwinner, female housewife — provides capitalism with 'two for the price of one'.
- Socialist feminists also stress the role of women as a 'reserve army of labour' in the event of an expansion of production such as in war.

10 For radical feminists, 'patriarchy' means male dominance, beginning in the private sphere.

11 Writers such as Kate Millett and Shulamith Firestone argue that patriarchy — where the male is head of the household — in the personal and private sphere of home and family, has always been the first and most important power relationship in the human social system — hence their famous slogan, 'the personal is political'.

12 'Sex' refers to the biological differences between men and women, including the capacity to bear children; while 'gender' is the cultural, social stereotypical role ascribed to them by society. Radical feminists especially argue that, while sexual differences are (more or less) fixed, gender roles are just a matter of social conditioning and can therefore be changed. In short, biology is *not* destiny.

13

Liberal feminism	Marxist feminism
Individualist	Collectivist
Reformist	Revolutionary
Denies the concept of class	Class inequality is primary problem

14

Liberal feminism	Radical feminism
Individualist	Collectivist — sisterhood
Reformist	Revolutionary
Focuses on public sphere	Focuses on private sphere

15

Marxist feminism	Radical feminism
Patriarchy begins in public, economic sphere	Patriarchy begins in private sphere
Class inequality is primary problem	Sexual inequality is primary problem
Class revolution	Sexual revolution

16 Traditional conservatives subscribe to the organic model of society, which portrays class, gender and even racial inequalities as natural, inevitable and desirable.

17 'Post-feminism' describes the view that feminism has done its job so effectively that it is now obsolete.

18 Three problems or criticisms of feminism:

- Anti-feminists, such as traditional conservatives and fascists, believe that gender hierarchy is natural, functional, inevitable and desirable.
- Some commentators — usually conservative journalists, whether male or female — have argued that feminism has done its job so effectively that it is now obsolete.
- Arguably, feminists have damaged their own cause by their internal divisions and — for some — their extremism, which has allowed simplistic stereotyping by their critics.

Chapter 7

1 'Ecologism' embraces deep ecology — ecocentric — and shallow ecology — anthropocentric; whereas 'environmentalism' is usually synonymous with shallow ecologism.

2 Ernst Haeckel (1879).

3 Rachel Carson (1962).

4 Holism is the belief that the natural world can only be understood as a whole, by studying the complex and interdependent relationships among its parts.

5 Toxic wastes, acid rain, the greenhouse effect, depletion of the ozone layer, global warming, globalisation, and growing concerns over food safety, genetically modified foods and pollution.

6 Anthropocentrism is the belief that human interests are of primary importance; the opposite of ecocentrism.

7 Ecocentrism is the belief that the ecological interests of the planet are of primary importance; the opposite of anthropocentrism.

8 Another word for 'ecocentric' is 'biocentric'.

9 Arne Naess (1972).

10 John Locke (1632–1704) expressed the anthropocentric view of shallow ecology.

11 Environmentalist critics of industrialism argue that its noxious effluents have had a damaging impact upon the ecosystem.

12 Light greens deal with the effects, but not the causes, of ecological crises. — e.g. investment in low-carbon technologies, and environmental taxes e.g. on air flights.

13 Dark greens are radical anthropocentrics who seek to address the causes of ecological problems, e.g. by cutting car use and air flights.

14 'Hard' ecology takes a scientific approach whereas 'soft' ecology takes a more spiritual/ethical approach.

15 Ethical issues raised by ecologism include:

- Animal rights and welfare.
- Concern for the interests of future generations.
- Biocentric equality and the intrinsic value of nature.

16 Three right-wing schools of ecologism are:

- Traditional conservatism.
- Nazism.
- Eco-capitalism.

Three left-wing schools of ecologism are:

- Eco-socialism.
- Eco-anarchism.
- Eco-feminism.

17 Organicism and the preservation of traditional ways of life link traditional conservatism to rural conservation.

18 Neo-liberals believe that the competitive and dynamic free market will provide innovative technological solutions to environmental problems.

19 Deep ecologists view eco-socialism as anti-ecological because it is anthropocentric.

20 Social ecology is the anarchist theory that human society should operate according to ecological principles, implying a belief in natural harmony and the need for a balance between humans and nature.

21 Mary Daly.

Chapter 8

1 'Multiculturalism' is a descriptive term for racial, ethnic, cultural and linguistic diversities within a society, and/or a normative term for the positive endorsement of cultural diversity.

2 The term 'multiculturalism' was first used in Canada in 1965 to describe an accepting and encouraging approach to bilingualism within the country.

3 Cultural diversity has been enhanced by increased migration due to:

- the need for new workers in a time of economic boom;
- a wave of refugees due to wars and the break-up of states like the Soviet Union and Yugoslavia;
- economic globalisation.

4 Some believe that multicultural policies can keep extremism at bay, but others believe that multiculturalism may allow or legitimise extremism.

5 'Post-colonialism' refers to assertions of cultural identity after independence of former colonies; examples:

- Gandhi's Indian nationalism.
- 1960s' black nationalism.
- Edward Said's book *Orientalism* (1978).

6 Identity politics refers to the pursuit of group interests defined by collective identity and common experience (for example, of culture, race or gender).

7 The collectivism and particularism of identity politics challenge the individualism and universalism of liberalism.

8 Minority rights are the individual and especially collective entitlements of marginalised groups in society.

9 Minority rights are controversial because:

- They may hinder integration of cultural groups into wider society.
- Positive discrimination is often perceived as unfair and counter-productive.
- There are inevitable tensions between minority group rights and individual rights.

10 Cultural diversity may be controversial because:

- It may weaken people's sense of their own cultural identity.
- It may undermine social stability or political unity.

11 Liberal multiculturalism embodies rationalism, freedom of choice and tolerance.

12 Criticisms of liberal multiculturalism include:

- It is contradictory because the liberal emphasis on individual rights conflicts with multiculturalism's emphasis on group rights.
- Liberal tolerance is limited and not morally neutral.
- Some critics regard liberal multiculturalism as a superficial 'celebration of costumes, customs and cooking'.

13 Pluralist multiculturalism goes further than liberal multiculturalism in accepting the equal validity and legitimacy of liberal, non-liberal and illiberal ideas and values.

14 Moral pluralism may be premised on moral indifference, which may be 'dangerous'.

15 Cosmopolitanism and multiculturalism are essentially conflicting ideas because cosmopolitanism believes in international or global identity transcending particular cultures.

16 Conservatives believe that security-seeking individuals and a stable society require cultural homogeneity.

17 Socialists criticise the emphasis on cultural identity because it cuts across class consciousness.

18 Dilemmas for liberal multiculturalism include:

- Multiculturalism is collectivist and, therefore, conflicts with liberal individualism.
- Its emphasis on the value of diversity and particularism conflicts with liberal universalism.
- Certain forms of multiculturalism may also impinge on human rights and freedoms, or on toleration.

19 Feminists object to patriarchal forms of culture.